Living God's Life

W.J. Caywood

ISBN 978-1-63903-797-1 (paperback)
ISBN 978-1-63903-798-8 (digital)

Christian Faith Publishing, Inc.
832 Park Avenue
Meadville, PA 16335
www.christianfaithpublishing.com

Unless otherwise identified, all Scripture quotations in this publication are from the New Revised Standard Version, copyright ©1989, Division of Christian Education of the National Council of Churches of Christ in the United States of America.

Printed in the United States of America

To Father Brandon Filbert, who, in becoming my spiritual
father, walked with me into the merciful arms of the
Lord Jesus and introduced me to the Father's love and
the path of communion in the blessed Holy Spirit.

Contents

Introduction

I have been drawn back to the biblical text of 2 Peter again and again over the last twenty or so years. The invaluable knowledge and wisdom gleaned from studying this letter and reflecting upon its practical import for myself is difficult to gauge. The spiritual fruit, which has come from both the study and subsequent teaching to others from this letter, has led me to the conclusion that the message(s) here need to be widely disseminated.

This book is my attempt to share what seems to be the most pertinent knowledge I have gained and benefited from while seeking to heed the apostle Peter's message and pressing into living in a way which is honoring to God. I wrote this because of an urgent inner compulsion and because God directed me to articulate and explain for others' sake what I have learned. That labor of writing is my attempt to be obedient to God.

The overarching purpose of this book is to state, as clearly and succinctly as possible, the basics of living moment-by-moment and day-by-day in the reality of the kingdom of God as manifested on earth. Thus, the tenor of this work is unapologetically theological while also simultaneously practical. My goal is to expound upon various aspects of experiencing being the disciple ("learner") of the Lord Jesus Christ, and thus living now in the Father's kingdom as the Holy Spirit operates on earth prior to our Lord's promised return.

The core conviction that undergirds the book is this: If those who identify themselves as believers in God through the Lord Jesus Christ obey God from the heart, in both word and deed, then many of the maladies afflicting the churches' relational health and witness will be healed. One of the surest signs of disease afflicting the church today is the divorce of what Christians say they believe, and the actual manner in which they make decisions and lead their lives. I propose that God has provided a way out of that sickly trap for his people in his written Word and, more specifically, in the second letter of Peter.

One of the foundational problems underlying this disparity between aspiring to acknowledge God's truth and actually doing what is righteous is an interior split in believer's hearts between "truth" (explored through theological reflection) and "wisdom" (found in the experiential adventure of being Christ's disciple). This deadly split must be ended for the church to be healthy, and it must happen in each of our hearts in order for us, together, to step up into God's glorious purpose for us in this generation. For this to happen, we must first recognize this sin, owning and lamenting for ourselves, and renounce the choices to live in this double-mindedness so the Spirit can heal us. The divine healing of the Spirit is available to all who ask and are willing to fully cooperate with the transforming power of grace.

During the writing process for this book, I have come to understand what a delicate task it is to balance these dual considerations: Speaking clearly on the doctrinal and theological truths taught in Scripture, and also expounding the practical implications of that truth for our actual attitudes and conduct. I am under no illusions about the difficulty of effectively addressing the great divide between truth and reality in people's actual experience—as though the content of this little book addresses every situation or need for readers. No, the blessed Spirit must do his excellent work in us. I have done what I can, consciously subjecting myself to the authority of Scripture in the same ways that I prescribe to the readers.

The content of the book is based upon a careful exposition of the letter of 2 Peter, taken as a whole and carefully considered in the context of the rest of Scripture. The goal has been to allow the content of the apostles' teaching in this letter, along with other sections of Scripture that speak to the same subjects—to guide, inform, and shape the reflections, questions, and answers that are proposed therein. I have ventured into this task knowing that "whatever was written in former days was written for our instruction, so that by steadfastness and by the encouragement of the scriptures we might have hope" (Romans 15:4).

I claim no originality in the interpretations presented of the biblical text or the proposed applications of it. I am deeply indebted to Christian theologians and interpreters from various times in church history. I recognize that God is the author of all things, including my very life and the Scriptures I have ventured into interpreting and making applications from. I have attempted to avoid any excessive speculation or to go beyond what the language of the text specifically refers to or seems to parallel with in other portions of Scripture. Further, my aim has been to make this book accessible to the reader, to avoid technical scholarly verbiage, and retain a level of serious inquiry into the biblical text. I leave it to critical readers to judge if I have succeeded in this.

I trust that God will be faithful to his people and utilize this work to richly bless many. To the degree that my goals are not met, I trust that God will be faithful to spur on others to search beyond what I have written for insight and understanding from the Lord. And above all, that many would search out for ways to heal this tragic divide in their own lives, and then teach and counsel their brothers and sisters in the Lord to do the same. The effectiveness of the witness of the church depends upon whether we delve deep into God's revealed truth and learn to obey the blessed Spirit as the Lord's disciples. In this abandonment to the living God, we can find the secret to avoiding being "unfruitful in the knowledge of our Lord Jesus Christ" (2 Peter 1:8).

CHAPTER 1

The Boldness of Humility
(2 Peter 1:1–4)

"What holds true of all spiritual truth is specially true of the abiding in Christ: *We must live and experience truth in order to know it.* Life-fellowship with Jesus is the only school for the science of heavenly things."[1]

What we do when greeting someone communicates much more about us than merely what we say. If we have been paying attention, we have all seen examples of the disparity between the words uttered and the behavior of the person speaking. We also intuitively recognize the genuineness and sincerity of the person whose body language agrees with his or her words. This innate human ability to recognize relational congruity also holds true for written correspondence—especially if it is personal communication.

What do the words we read in 2 Peter show us about the author? The simplicity of his introductory wording reveals much about his simplicity, sincerity, and the love of God, which had so powerfully transformed him. Note that Peter simply stated his name along with the descriptive title, "apostle"—the holy task to which he had been called by the Lord Jesus. The opening follows the standard ancient literary conventions; however, the content of these opening sentences expresses the richness of his experience in faith.

Also observe that he uses the name "Simeon (or Simon) Peter," and that he speaks of himself as "a servant of Jesus Christ" (v. 1). The Greek term he used here is *doulos* and can also be translated as "slave" or "bond servant." Why not simply begin with "Peter, an apostle of Jesus Christ" (1 Peter 1:1)? Why introduce himself as a "servant" first, and then "apostle"? The answer lies deep within his life experience as a disciple of Jesus, whom he proclaimed as Lord and Messiah (Acts 2:36).

Peter is the man to whom Jesus, upon first meeting him, said, "You are Simon son of John," and then declared, as though it was a matter of fact, "You are to be called Cephas [i.e. Peter, or "rock"]" (John 1:42). Upon seeing nets overflowing with fish under the simple instruction of Jesus, he was overcome, and he exclaimed, "Go away from me, Lord, for I am a sinful man!" (Luke 5:8) He was among the first of those who left their trade as fishermen when summoned by Jesus to be his disciple (Mark 1:16–20).

Again and again, in the gospel accounts, Peter is the most outspoken among Jesus's chosen twelve—the first to speak boldly of the faith and even challenge the Lord's words (Mark 8:29, 31–32; Matthew 16:15–23). He seems to have often spoken up for the rest of the group when Jesus's teaching perplexed or shocked them (Mark 10:28; John 6:66–69). He alone among the terrified disciples actually invited himself to walk on open water with Jesus, and then actually did so, shortly before sinking (Matthew 14:28–31)! Jesus chose him and two others to witness the transfiguring of his body on the mountain (Mark 9:1–8).

It was Peter who voiced an objection to having the Lord wash his feet like a household slave and then insisted that he give him a bath (John 13:6–10)! He was the one who boldly proclaimed a solemn intention to suffer and die with Jesus, only to deny that he knew him three times just hours later (Luke 22:33–34). It was Peter that the angels at the tomb specifically named in delivering the good news of Jesus being raised from the dead (Mark 16:7) and to whom the Lord himself appeared (Luke 24:34; 1 Corinthians 15:5). And it was to Peter that the Lord asked the stinging question, "Simon son of John, do you love me?" three times—once for each of his prior denials—in order to warn and commission him for the work he had been given (John 21:15–19).

The readers were very familiar with Peter's turbulent and inconsistent behavior as Jesus's disciple. And now, they also knew him as a man who had been transformed by the grace of the Spirit. Thus, they knew well that they could trust his words because of his consistently demonstrated humility as a slave of the Lord Jesus Christ.

Peter addresses the letter to "those who have received a faith as precious as ours through the righteousness of our God and Savior Jesus Christ" (v. 1). He understood how precious the "faith" is because he had learned to live by faith in God through the Lord Jesus (1 Peter 1:3, 21). The God he dared to trust initiated and nourished Peter's own faith "through the righteousness" of Christ. What is "the righteousness" of Christ? Perhaps other passages of Scripture can help us here.

Peter publicly proclaimed Jesus as "the Holy and Righteous One" (Acts 3:14) in the days following Pentecost.[2] To speak of Jesus as "righteous" is to refer to his divine nature, his character as holy, and his mission in the world as the One who suffered on behalf of others to make them righteous (Isaiah 53:11; 1 Peter 3:18).[3] Along with Peter, other New Testament authors assert that in the person of Messiah Jesus ("God and Savior"), the righteous character and nature of God was manifested, the mission of redemptive suffering was completed, and the way to authentic spiritual maturity was secured on behalf of all who would come to him in faith.[4]

The "righteousness of our God and Savior Jesus Christ" (v. 2) had a transforming impact on Peter's whole person. He learned the way of Christ through faith in the Holy One, who gives those who believe "righteousness" and power to practice thoughts and behavior pleasing to God. Thus, he could speak authoritatively of receiving "a faith as precious as ours through" (v. 1) the One he loves and serves because it was a living reality to him.

Simon Peter also speaks a blessing upon his readers. Those who have experienced the mercy of God and who seek to serve God by serving others in the kingdom of God have a unique ability to bless others. These blessings are not mere formality or polite gesture. The blessing of Peter is a bold statement that is both powerful and rich in meaning because it is infused with living faith in the risen Jesus.

Take careful note of the contents of the blessings: Notice that each word of Peter's blessing references an aspect of the work of Jesus Christ as he sits at the right hand of God the Father.[5] The "knowledge of God and Jesus the Lord" (v. 2) is the source of the abundance of grace and peace that he speaks over his hearers. In other words, the blessings of grace and peace are given and received through such knowledge of God. Life is a gift of grace, and peace is the manifestation of God's Spirit dwelling within a believing person.

It is important to state the source of such spiritual blessings namely because the blessings are such that they can come *only* from right-standing, intimate relationship with God. A personal and intimate knowledge of the Creator is essential for human beings to become who they were created to be and to authentically love other people. Human beings who live spiritually separated from their Creator are like fish swimming in water, who think that they should be on the shore. They become so convinced and determined that they do not belong in the water that they literally kill themselves to get onto the land where they cannot breathe! Contrary to such insanity is the grace and peace that comes from God. It is this life-giving blessing that Peter passes in abundance to his readers.

Peter knew and preached the reality of the good news, both with his words and by the way he lived his life. Thus, the opening description and blessing are squarely centered on the person of God and on Jesus Christ, whom he served. Peter wanted all to see and know the beauty and excellences of the Lord's character and love extended in the gospel.

With this background in mind, perhaps we can now begin to hear the succinct description given of the marvelous truth about God and human beings that follows (vv. 3–4) with clearer and richer insight. Each aspect of the God-given blessings that Peter reveals here require prayerful consideration in order to be understood. We will briefly consider them each one-by-one, and then together as a whole.

First, through the Lord Jesus, "divine power has given us everything needed for life and godliness" (v. 3). All of scripture explicitly or implicitly testifies to this assertion, namely that the almighty Creator is the source of all things. Everything that exists was created by the will of God.[6] Thus, the provision made by Jesus Christ of "everything needed for life and godliness" (v. 3) is a gift from our "faithful Creator" (1 Peter 4:19).

There is marvelous simplicity in this statement. The maker of the heavens and earth has given those who have faith all that they need to be faithful to God in this life! This is an echo of the Lord's promise that if God's people pursue "his kingdom and the righteous way in which it is governed,"[7] all that they need will be provided.

Second, the "divine power" and provision of "everything needed" has come to us through "the knowledge of him who called us" (v. 3). Our attention here is turned to the person of God, who calls all people to repentance and faith in Jesus. The response of "an honest and good heart" (Luke 8:15) to the gospel is the only way that a person can truly and effectually have knowledge of God. This personal encounter brings the knowledge of God and Jesus Christ, His Son. Yet what kind of knowledge is this?

It's spiritual, experiential, and transformative personal knowledge of the character and love of God. Peter noted elsewhere, "Although you have not seen him, you love him; and even though you do not see him now, you believe in him and rejoice with an indescribable and glorious joy, for you are receiving the outcome of your faith, the salvation of your souls" (1 Peter 1:8–9). Mere intellectual reasoning, affirmations, or philosophical speculation about God, however valid or helpful, are surpassed in this kind of knowledge. To know God in this way requires one to heed and engage the Person of the risen Lord Jesus with one's whole heart and life. True knowledge of God always entails a progressive transformation of one's whole person by the inner working and indwelling of God's Spirit, and this manifests in a person's actions.

Third, we read that God's "call" comes "by [or 'through'] his own glory and goodness" (v. 3) to those who exercise faith in Jesus Christ. Peter seems to have assumed that his readers shared a basic living knowledge of God's self-revelation within the Scripture. To understand this notion as modern readers, it is helpful to consider what the Scriptures reveal about God's attributes.

The terms "glory" and "goodness" describe what is revealed elsewhere in Scripture as God's power and character.[8] The primary sense of the word "glory" as applied to God "denotes the revelation of God's being, nature, and presence" to humankind.[9] "Glory" describes "the majesty and eminence that radiates from God's own being."[10] The provision of "life and godliness" and "knowledge" to the people of God has always come by revelation through a manifestation of God's "glory." Peter is asserting that God has called people to faith out of the sheer generosity of his nature for the sake of demonstrating his glory, honor, and great love among his creatures.[11] The Lord Jesus desires all to embrace his passionate invitation of love and to have right-standing relationship with their Creator restored freely.[12]

Fourth, "he has given us...his precious and very great promises" so that we "may escape" the corrupting power of lust and "may become participants of the divine nature" (v. 4). Of all the statements in this text, this is surely the most far-reaching. Those familiar with the Bible might ordinarily expect to hear about promises concerning the "glory and goodness" of God, God's provision of salvation, or the invitation to faith in the divine Messiah, but perhaps less so that we can now become "partakers" of God's very nature! Even so, Peter is not the first one to describe the relationship between Jesus and his disciples in terms like this. The same concept is expressed in the Lord's teachings and elsewhere in the New Testament with different metaphors.[13] The level of intimacy God desires with his people is truly profound!

The challenge of Peter's final effort to remind and encourage believers to live with wholehearted faith in the Lord Jesus is fundamentally about exhorting them to be connected to God in consistently close and intimate ways. This partaking in relationship with God is at the core of exercising faith as Jesus himself taught us to do, and indeed which he left us a perfect example of how to do. It is this radical teaching and practice that sets Peter and the other New Testament authors apart from other "false teachers" in making claims to divine inspiration. At the core of obedience to God, which makes the apostles' teaching trustworthy, is the intimate relationship they had with God, verified by boldly living out of strength and passion from God's indwelling Spirit.

The terminology that most self-identified Christians use to describe their relationship to God can sadly often come across as abstract and detached when devoid of this notion of "partaking of the divine nature." For example, one may call oneself a "worshipper of God" or "servant of Christ" or even "friend of God." These are biblical terms and concepts; however, when spoken in isolation from the primary metaphor of how we relate to God through Christ Jesus by the Holy Spirit, they are inadequate and can even be misleading because they can easily be misunderstood to be impersonal in nature and practice.

To bear truthful witness of God's love, we must first know him intimately by "abiding" or "partaking of the divine nature," and secondly, demonstrate it consistently by how we live. Notably, we relate to God as blood-bought persons who are learning to be disciples of Jesus Christ, and the journey is not always perfectly straight. We can and do sin in different ways. Yet even so, the believer who is a partaker of intimate relationship with God may "fall seven times" but still "rise again" (Proverbs 24:16).

Amazingly, even the imperfections of God's people who wholeheartedly obey him bear positive witness to his love because the unbeliever will see an honest life being radically transformed by God's power, even in the midst of spiritual and emotional brokenness. To the unbeliever, the effects of God's love overflowing in the life of a believer are attractive and desirable, like "salt" or "light." This was the chief purpose of the Lord's self-sacrifice—to make it possible for us to be united together with him as "living stones" that make up God's household (1 Peter 2:4–10), to be united with God, and to bring hope to the dying world! So let us go boldly forward into apprenticeship of learning how to be a "partaker" of God's life now, and thus join in being the means by which God blesses others throughout our lives on earth.

God speaks through Peter's letter with authority because Peter exercised his position of authority and responsibility as an apostle of

Christ for others' sake—consciously aware of his equality with "those who have received" this precious faith (v. 1). This radical humility of servanthood (imitating his Savior), expressed in the simple profession of a shared faith, demonstrates that Peter is a man who understands the costs of being a disciple of the Lord Jesus and the wisdom necessary to practice it. Let us then listen to our brother Peter and be blessed by obeying his exhortations as God's word.

CHAPTER 2

Being Partakers of God (2 Peter 1:1–4)

"The greater your knowledge of God becomes, the more you will realize the magnitude of his promises. When God blesses us, he changes our very being so that whatever we were by nature is transformed by the gift of his Holy Spirit, so that we may truly become partakers of his nature."[1]

The opening section of Peter's letter, while carrying a dignified and simple message, also has extraordinary implications for us. These assertions fundamentally challenge how we think about God and reality. Therefore, I think it is necessary to give an extended reflection upon them.

Arguably, the loftiest thoughts of human beings in all of history involve the many attempts to comprehend and explain the mystery of how the Divine Being relates to created things. Depending upon which religion and/or philosophy one consults, the answers vary widely. However, each of the historic world religions has always sought to answer this same basic question: "How does God (or the Ultimate) relate to created things—especially human beings?"

At the center of the Lord Jesus's teaching is an answer to this basic question as well. However, the Lord's answer is unique when compared to all other philosophical and religious systems devised in human history. Simply put, Jesus asserted that God created humans to know and love himself by partaking of God's nature. However,

19

the corrupting power of sin destroys our ability to know and love God. God's provision in Jesus Christ frees us from sin so that we can experientially know God and receive power for "life and godliness."

The Lord's chosen disciples became convinced of this teaching, and they then echoed it in their own teachings as well. The opening of the letter is an example of Peter's rephrasing of Christ's claim about himself: "I came that they may have life, and have it abundantly" (John 10:10).

Peter also amplified the Lord's words by describing redeemed humans as "partakers" of God's nature. The image of "partaking" seems to convey that faith in Jesus Christ involves a mysterious uniting with the living Lord in spirit, thus sharing in God's actual divine life. In fact, this sharing is so intimate that his very life, the life of the divine nature, becomes our life, and it provides the means to become free from sin.[2] The mystery is in fact so great that Peter was only able to describe it with the metaphor of this active receiving and sharing.

Peter's highly descriptive and rich language also reveal to us that his readers were already aware of the great mysteries he was elaborating upon. The most important of the premises Peter elaborates upon is the foundational knowledge that God desires that all people live in intimate relationship with him by faith. The Scriptures testify often to God's desire for his human creatures to willingly obey him by leading holy and righteous lives—filled with and founded upon his love. For example, Peter says elsewhere to believers: "Finally, all of you, have unity of spirit, sympathy, love for one another, a tender heart, and a humble mind" (1 Peter 3:8).

Another bit of foundational knowledge Peter's readers had is that the most basic obstacle to human fellowship and right relating to God is embedded within the human heart—that is "lust" (or "passions") born from within oneself. Peter does not elaborate on this point beyond asserting that we must escape the "lust" that is corrupting God's creation. His emphasis is upon who God is and what God has done to make it possible for us to be delivered from ourselves and the overwhelming influence of the world system that reinforces our inclination to sin. We generally like to pin blame on some exterior thing, environmental influence, or person for our problems.

However, the Lord and his apostles point that the human dilemma of being alienated from God is rooted in the human soul itself. The apostle John describes the many facets of this obstacle:

"Do not love the world or the things in the world. The love of the Father is not in those who love the world; for all that is in the world—the desire of the flesh, the desire of the eyes, the pride in riches—comes not from the Father but from the world" (1 John 2:15–16).

Lust (or "passions") is the most lethal enemy of human beings and is the motivation that leads to sin, which separates us from God. The dead set rebellion of the human self (i.e., "the flesh") against one's Creator due to the effects of sin on creation can only be adequately dealt with by genuine repentance, relinquishment of self-life, and conscious self-denial for God's sake. Lust is the natural expression of a dead spirit and the driving force behind human idolatry, so naturally, it is unbefitting in the life of a believer. Any expressions of coveting or greed in human life fall under the term "lust" or "passions"—an insatiable, self-serving appetite for material things, religious or political power, or sensual or "spiritual" experiences.[3]

Peter and the writers of Scripture assume that sin violently separates us from God and makes it impossible for us to experience living connected to God's life. In his previous letter, he had made it plain: Until we are set right with God through the blood of the Lord Jesus Christ, we have no hope of enjoying God's good fellowship and eternal gifts (1 Peter 1:18–21). Until we are cleansed and forgiven in Christ by the power of the Holy Spirit, we cannot begin to learn to be holy as God is holy (1 Peter 1:13–17). Until we are healed of our waywardness of heart and given a reborn heart to love God, we cannot truly love people (1 Peter 1:22–23).

Peter's brief set of assertions about God and Jesus the Messiah are like a written shorthand describing for his readers the glory and mystery of God's grace to fully meet human needs with divine provision. Let us carefully consider these assertions one-by-one in more detail.

First, we need "everything…for life and godliness" (v. 3). We are simply incapable of living the kind of lives for which we were designed by our Creator if we stand alienated from him. The entire biblical record of God's acts of deliverance for his creation and people instructs that we must be delivered and provided for by God, our Creator and Savior.[4] Self-sufficiency is an illusion of human pride. God has created us to be dependent upon him, and he has generously given us all that we need in the Lord Jesus Christ, whose spirit lives within us and gives us life.

Second, we need and can have "knowledge of him [God] who called us" (v. 3). The distinctive trait of the "God of Abraham, Isaac, and Jacob" (Exodus 3:13–15) is that he speaks to all people and has never left himself without a witness. Yet he especially speaks to those who exercise faith. The authors of the Scripture lived by faith and had encountered God themselves or believed in the testimony of others who had heard God's voice. This is why Peter confidently proclaimed that God patiently works to bring people "to repentance" (2 Peter 3:9) so that they can experience the transformative power of the Gospel.

Third, everything that we have received has been gifted through God's "divine power" and "knowledge" (v. 3); and thus, we have the "precious and very great promises" of God (v. 4). The effect of receiving the promises is that we are able to escape the destructive consequences of lust and actually become "partakers of the divine nature" (v. 4 RSV)! These two distinct points made about redeemed people are intimately interconnected.

Again, lust and its accompanying corruption of mind and emotions are the fundamental problems that prevent humans from being able to become "partakers" in God. We were made for noble purposes, but our inclination toward idolatry pervert and prevent our God-given needs and desires for communion with God and other people to be met. Human beings have two options for fulfilling their deepest needs for community: either authentic communion with one's Creator in the church, or the false and empty alternatives of different forms of "lust," which never actually fulfill the need but only temporarily numb it.

If we are honest, we must admit that the radical nature of this teaching is quite disturbing to the mere human intellect, and even offensive to our dearly cherished notions of deity. There are many professing Christians today who are exactly like those early followers of Jesus, who grumbled and left him after he proclaimed:

> Very truly, I tell you, unless you eat the flesh of the Son of Man and drink his blood, you have no life in you... Those who eat my flesh and drink my blood abide in me, and I in them. Just as the living Father sent me, and I live because of the Father, so whoever eats me will live because of me. (John 6:53, 56–57)

To the "fleshly" mind, these words of Jesus sound insane! However, it is not only because it seems irrational and grotesque, but more so because we prefer a kind of God that we can keep at a manageable distance and retain the illusion of self-autonomy as we try to maneuver through our lives. At the heart of this biblical teaching is the stark illustration that one must give up one's comfortable conceptions of spiritual living to actually relate to God on his terms.

In conclusion, there are also two basic truths that can be gleaned from these words of the apostle regarding God's grace to us in the Lord Jesus.[5] First, why have we been given this marvelous provision of life and godliness in the knowledge of Jesus Christ? This divine gift is for the "glory of God" and comes from the sheer "goodness" of God for the good of his creatures. Second, what Peter asserts about the nature of the gift of life and godliness is that it is also simply beyond human ability to fully comprehend. We can become "partakers" in God's nature because we bear the "image and likeness of God" (Genesis 1:26–27) and have the gift to choose to respond to the merciful and gracious embrace of God.

God wants us to genuinely love him! However, how all this is actually possible is beyond the scope of human comprehension, and thus, it requires faith to embrace the truth. The means of "working out our salvation" (Philippians 2:12) can never simply be reduced to a mere acceptance of Christ's death or an intellectual or emotional affirmation of the Christian creeds. Rather, we must participate in our salvation by actually relating to God in accord with God's desire to indwell and fill the whole of our nature and persons. To love God entails continually opening oneself by faith to the One who is holy and to love and engage in the holy task of abstaining "from the desires of the flesh that wage war against the soul" (1 Peter 2:11). This is how a believing person escapes "from the corruption that is in the world because of lust" (v. 4).

CHAPTER 3

Obedience of Faith (2 Peter 1:5–7)

"Truth is always a quarry hard to hunt, and therefore we must look everywhere for its tracks. The acquisition of true religion is just like that of crafts; both grow bit by bit; apprentices must despise nothing. If a man despise the first elements as small and insignificant, he will never reach the perfection of wisdom."[1]

After describing God's grace and gift of spiritual life in the Lord Jesus in succinct and exalted terms, Peter turned his reader's attention to the effect that faith in Christ is to have on their lives. For Peter, like all the other writers of the Scripture, truth was never merely abstract or theoretical but intensely practical. For them, the most exalted descriptions of God's being and work were meant to inspire God's people to worship, love, and obey God in the concrete circumstances of life.

The particular ways that God the Spirit utilizes life circumstances for this transforming work within us varies from person to person. The interior process of transformation, however, does have a very definite pattern that applies to all believing persons. This process can be roughly sketched out as follows: After one has been given God's new life within, one is responsible to learn to exercise faith in response to the dynamic, supernatural work of breaking down and reshaping by the Holy Spirit. This involves the enjoyment of the goodness of God and renouncing self-life and the love of the things of the world.[2] The dynamic flow of spiritual maturation must be expressed in skilled practice of "righteousness" in relationship to other people.[3]

Faith (or trust) in the God revealed in Jesus Christ and Scripture is the starting point for all authentic spiritual growth into full human maturation. Indeed, without faith, no one can know or please God. The truth revealed by Jesus must transform and inform everything one thinks and does; the content of one's faith must define how one sees the world. Thus this series of exhortations is to be acted on because of the grace of God and the offer of becoming "partakers of the divine nature" (v. 4 RSV).

The apostle Peter has helped his readers to learn how to actively participate in their own spiritual maturation by giving a short list of particular character qualities and outward signs of righteousness that are essential to someone's transformation. These are not how-to steps to becoming godly but rather descriptive markers of what godliness should and can look like in person's life as they are being transformed.

First, notice that the apostle gave a command to his readers to "supplement" (v. 5 RSV) or "support" their faith because of the facts he had just stated (vv. 3–4). Thus, believers are to consciously and diligently choose to order their lives in ways that accord with the faith. Faith, by itself, is incomplete without the developing of virtue, moral character, and positive disciplines in one's life.[4] What Peter seemed to be urging here is for all to diligently pursue holiness in life because the eternal life promised in the Gospel demands that all who have faith to "be holy yourselves in all your conduct" (1 Pet 1:15; cf. 3:8–12).[5] Faith, then, is to be built upon by a succession of virtues or godly character traits: goodness, knowledge, self-control, endurance, godliness, mutual familial affection, and lastly, love.

The first term, "goodness," can also be translated as "virtue" or "moral excellence."[6] The primary sense in which the term was used in the Greek translation of Scripture then currently used (LXX or Septuagint) always refers to the being and character of God and his acts; God "is the arbiter and judge, as he is the norm and standard, of creaturely goodness."[7] The "goodness" of God is also connected to God's faithfulness to his covenant[8] and his promises (cf., 2 Peter 1:3).

Because God is uniquely "good," it necessarily follows that those who claim to believe are to excel in moral "goodness" or virtuous character as well as defined by God.[9] Thus Peter exhorted them to develop interior excellence of character, which is expressed in a life of integrity and vigorous zeal for righteousness.

Next, we are to supplement our moral excellence with "knowledge." The kind of knowledge Peter has in mind is knowledge of God—learning that leads to experiential familiarity and love of one's Creator, not mere head knowledge. Knowledge of God is always connected in the Scriptures to wisdom and the "fear" of God.[10] True knowledge of God is essential to beginning and living out covenant relationship with God.[11] To know God is to live in wholeness and integrity—to be humble, open, generous, and faithful.

Knowledge of God and his will are to be supported with the practice of "self-control" (or self-restraint), the restraint or control of one's impulses or desires or simply to be self-disciplined.[12] To learn how to be in command of one's appetites or desires rather than enslaved to them is essential for obtaining wisdom that comes from the fear of God. Self-control that is pleasing to God is a response of faith, supported by virtue and enlightened by knowledge of God. To understand the necessity and practice of self-control is a sign of wisdom; one knows the consequences of one's actions and their origin in the heart and soul. The persons who practice self-control know what true goodness is and desire it above all else.[13] One who restrains and denies the desires of the flesh (self-life) does so in order not to lose what really matters in this life and that to come.[14]

Complementary to self-restraint is "endurance"—perseverance or patience in affliction or trials. Here is an admonition to exercise fortitude under difficult circumstances, choosing to remain faithful to the confession of faith in Christ through suffering, persecution, and affliction.[15] The capacity for this kind of endurance in life is an undying hope and firm conviction in the goodness and trustworthiness of God and his word.[16] To endure is evidence that one can see with the "eyes of the heart" (Ephesians 1:18) beyond the present circumstances to the One who stands and walks with us. Christ is our hope, model, and pioneer in all things for he himself learned to obey through the endurance of trials.[17]

An essential companion to endurance in trials is "godliness."[18] Godliness is an observable attribute of a person who has a heart attitude of awe and reverence for God,[19] emanating from a humble heart that knows God. True godliness is expressed in obedience, a desire to please God, and rejoicing in the truth. The Lord Jesus is the greatest example of how to do this.[20] Thus we know from the Lord's example that a godly person "fears God" and worships and serves him alone.

Next, Peter admonished his readers to supplement godliness with mutual familial affection for one another as brothers and sisters.[21] Here is an admonition to practice kindness, rooted in deeply felt affection for others as one should have within a family or among close friends. In this context, the people are the family of believers— the friends of Jesus (John 15:12–17)—who have come by faith to have intimate knowledge of God's love and trustworthy character. They are thus to love one another as equal heirs in the kingdom.[22] As in all of these character traits, Peter commended Jesus as the best example of how to identify with and love people[23] by empathizing, showing compassion, and inviting all who respond to find healing in the holy God of love and mercy.

The final supplement we are to add is "love," in the way God loves us—that is, *agape*. It means to esteem, have warm regard for, take an active interest in, and otherwise show love to people, regardless of who they are or how one knows them.[24] The Greek term *agape*, as used in the Greek translation of OT (LXX), describes the loving kindness of God (sense of OT term *hesed*) and carries with it concepts of God's covenant love and faithfulness to his chosen ones.[25] This love is to be given in return to God with joy and gratitude.[26] God's children are then to love as he loved—to love other believers and enemies[27]—because true faith apprehends God's love and thus, must have practical outworking towards other people.[28]

This is a remarkable listing, and these admonitions should be sobering to anyone who reflects upon them. What are the actual implications for our lives if we put these into practice? Here are a few observations to consider.

A person's faith is the inner reality that goodness is to support. Without faith, a person has no capability or resources, with which to craft a new life as a member of the people of God. Then knowledge is listed next in order to enlighten, guide, and sharpen one's understanding of God and what pleases him.

Self-control adds additional elements of power to discern and to live wisely with the knowledge one has of God. Endurance is the ability to choose to remain faithful through the inevitable difficulties, afflictions, and testing that one will endure in life.

Godliness is a constant progression into a fuller experience of reverencing God and being holy in the Holy Spirit. Mutual affection toward each other as members of God's family is the healthy expression of a heart devoted to God and his people. Lastly, love ends the listing because it is the mark of true spiritual maturity. Those who "love one another deeply from the heart" (1 Peter 1:22) know God and love others without fear of any person or creature in the world.

Peter clearly intended for his readers to put these admonitions into practice, but he does not elaborate on how we might go about doing that. Perhaps he refrained from giving specific instructions on how to do so for the same reasons other authors of Scripture often did so—to encourage each person to seek the guidance of the Holy Spirit. Thus, to apply these progressive movements to one's spiritual life, Peter seems to have meant for his readers to do simply what he instructed: Intentionally supplement "these things" to your faith and depend upon the Holy Spirit to instruct you about what specifically to do.

Now having stated that Peter did not give specific instructions for the "how" of doing this, I do think that there were indications in how Peter wrote that help us. First, there appears to be a definite progression in the listing; each one seems to build upon the other. Each one has a discernibly different character trait that, so to speak, works a different angle in the gradual reformation of the inner life of the believer. Also, it is telling that the listing begins with faith and ends with love (*agape*).

Love is the end goal, and thus, one can apply these admonitions in the following ways: These character traits all complement one another and form the essential building blocks of renewing the image of God within the believing person.

For example, the moral energy of virtue is necessary to propel us on into life-long learning in God's ways. The appropriation of "goodness" in one's soul assumes a growing knowledge of God's infinite covenant love. The purifying power of God in the human heart is evidenced in endurance through the most difficult of afflictions. While one is learning to exercise self-control, one is also learning to love a brother or sister in the Lord. As one's knowledge increases, so the need to practice self-control and endurance of trials is necessary for knowing how to appropriate the increased knowledge. And as one's reverence for God deepens, one will be faced with graver temptations to abandon loving one's brothers and sisters in Christ.

Finally, the crowning character trait of love (*agape*) towards God and other people is the end goal of faith for which we were called by God's "own glory and virtue" (v. 3).

> For the whole law is summed up in a single
> commandment, "You shall love your neighbor as
> yourself." (Galatians 5:14)

This is the chief mark of spiritual maturation in a human being.

How are we to "supplement" or "add to" our faith? I think that E. M. Bounds has provided the answer in asserting that Peter assumed that this could only be done "by constant, earnest praying. Thus faith is kept alive by prayer, and every step taken in this adding of grace to grace is accompanied by prayer."[29]

The reward for supplementing one's faith is quite great as Peter details in the following verses. Those who put into practice God's commandments and teach others to do the same "will be called great in the kingdom of heaven" (Matthew 5:19) and "will receive a rich welcome into the eternal kingdom of our Lord and Savior Jesus Christ" (v. 11).

CHAPTER 4

Rewards of Diligence (2 Peter 1:8–11)

"It is only when we introduce our own will into our relation to God that we get into trouble. When we weave into the pattern of our lives threads of our own selfish desires we instantly become subject to hindrances from the outside... If we find ourselves irked by external hindrances, be sure we are victims of our own self-will. Nothing can hinder the heart that is fully surrendered and quietly trusting, because nothing can hinder God."[1]

There are priceless treasures and sober warnings in this section of Peter's letter, which we dare not overlook or, worse, ignore. The form and progression of the words are simply stated but point to profound truth about what is required to grow up by grace into full human maturity. What he has left for all who have ears to hear is both a guide and an exhortation to loving obedience to the Lord Jesus. Let us listen attentively to the word of God.

In the context of the chapter, this passage is an elaboration on the purpose of the listing of "these things" (v. 8). He seems to have assumed that the readers understand what each one was and what was involved in learning how to actualize growth into these godly character traits. What he goes on to elaborate here is the reason for making them one's own. There seems to be at least several purposes either stated or implied in his words.

First, he asserts that "if these things [essentials for the development of godly character] are yours and are increasing among you, they will keep you from being ineffective and unfruitful in the knowledge of our Lord Jesus Christ" (v. 8). The double negative emphasis can be translated directly from Greek as "not unproductive nor unfruitful" (my translation). It seems that the wording here is significant: He was affirming the reciprocal effect of growing up spiritually through godly character development and avoiding becoming spiritually unfruitful. Thus, to put the matter another way, the practice of these disciplines will act to prevent a believing person from not living in the fullness of God's promises. Hindrances to the experiential practice of God's gift of eternal life in the present sojourn of faith are real. To emphasis the truth of what one can learn to grow up into spiritually, he has highlighted the opposite path one could take.

Second, what he merely implied (v. 8), he then explicitly states. The lack of "these things" in a person's life is a sign of spiritual near-sightedness and even blindness. Indeed, such a lifestyle betrays the fact that such a person has chosen not to remember the Lord's work of grace and his or her experience of the "cleansing of past sins" (v. 9). This kind of willful turning away from experientially known truth of God's grace in Christ is exceptionally foolish and dangerous to one's soul.

Scripture warns again and again of "remembering" God's covenant and his redeeming work and his commands. For example, the psalmist testifies:

> I will call to mind the deeds of the LORD; I will remember your wonders of old. I will meditate on all your work, and muse on your mighty deeds. Your way, O God, is holy. What god is so great as our God?" (Psalm 77:11–13)[2]

The whole of the New Testament witnesses to God's character and work of deliverance manifested in the Lord Jesus Christ. This testimony draws from and echoes the testimony of the Scriptures as a whole. God is the primary actor in Scripture and object of faith for those who believe his word given in history. Faith and its expression in righteous living are the main themes of God's word to his ancient people. The Lord Jesus confirmed and taught the same.

Following his Lord's example, Peter employed similar metaphors to describe the process of knowing and loving God by faith.[3] The primary word picture is that of spiritual "sight" on the one hand and "blindness" on the other. The Lord said:

> Your eye is the lamp of your body. If your eye is healthy, your whole body is full of light; but if it is not healthy, your body is full of darkness. Therefore consider whether the light in you is not darkness. If then your whole body is full of light, with no part of it in darkness, it will be as full of light as when a lamp gives you light with its rays. (Luke 11:34–36)

This word picture teaches essential truths about why human beings respond to the word of God—either in faith or unbelief. As Peter noted, those who lack "these things" show, by their lives, that they have chosen to forget "the cleansing of past sins" (v. 9). In doing this, they are also choosing not to remember God's mercy to them and not to fear the Lord God, who has the right and power to punish them or requite them for their sins. They have taken for granted the goodness and mercy of God. Further, this condition of being spiritually "nearsighted and blind" (v. 9) seems to be brought on by unbelief and a refusal to practice by faith the inner disciplines which he summarized earlier (vv. 5–7). By not remembering the truth that one does know about God—particularly the promise of forgiveness of sin and eternal life in the Gospel—a person practices self-deception.

The fact that someone can practice such self-deception is then a reason for his readers to ensure that they do not follow that path. For on the one hand, others' pious unbelief, manifested in their character and life, serves as a negative testimony in the face of the knowledge of God. On the other hand, the life affirming obedience in practicing "these things" (v. 8) opens up an extraordinary vision of the present reality of "[God's] precious and very great promises" (v. 4). The two possible roads one could take in the inner life should motivate his readers to "be all the more eager to confirm your [the readers'] call and election" (v. 10).

How are believers to "confirm your call and election" (v. 10)? What does this involve? How is this exhortation related to the other sections of the chapter we have already examined? The repetition of the phrase "these things" (v. 4, 8) I think can help us answer these questions.

The first use of the phrase "these things" (v. 4) refers to the gracious supernatural acts of God in Jesus Christ, which reveal the extraordinary character of God. This revelation of God's bountiful provision to redeemed humans shows us the heart of God and what pleases him above all else. This is God's action toward and on behalf of believers in Christ.

The second use of the phrase "these things" (v. 8) refers to the appropriate response of redeemed humans to this revelation of the character and will of God in the Person of Jesus Christ. This response requires engaging the whole person in a progressive conversion of one's beliefs, thought patterns, behavior, and stewardship. Nothing in life is to be held back from God's desire to transform and reform his people so they can reflect together his glory and goodness (2 Peter 1:3). Thus, apathy or resistance to conversion by individuals and groups of professing believers is simply out of character for those who do in fact know and love the triune God.

The practice of disciplines to develop godly character traits he briefly described (vv. 5–7) are the means by which the children of God are able to "confirm" that they have been called to "partake in the divine nature," (v. 4, RSV) and so escape the self-destruction of their own souls. To this, they are called by faith. The cultivation of the inner reality of "these things" and their outer expression in one's character and way of life confirm that a person belongs to God's people. This truth is affirmed in Scripture as a whole. For example, John the apostle flatly states:

> Now by this we may be sure that we know
> him, if we obey his commandments. Whoever

says, "I have come to know him," but does not
obey his commandments, is a liar, and in such
a person the truth does not exist; but whoever
obeys his word, truly in this person the love of
God has reached perfection. By this we may be
sure that we are in him: whoever says, "I abide
in him," ought to walk just as he walked. (1 John
2:3–6)[4]

Indeed, there is a profound difference between God's own people and unbelieving people who merely live and die in ignorance of
the one true God. That difference is captured in the term "election"
(v. 10). Simply stated, this refers to God's sovereign act of choosing
a people for himself from the whole human family in each succeed-
ing generation. The most prominent example is God's act of calling
and proclaiming promises to Abraham and his descendants.[5] Israel,
as God's chosen people, received divine revelation and favor as well
as punishment for disobedience according to stipulations of the
covenant Almighty God had made with them.[6] This covenant was
bestowed upon Israel for a particular purpose which was only par-
tially revealed to them.[7]

The eternal purpose of the covenant was kept secret in the heart
of God till the revelation of faith in Messiah Jesus was proclaimed—
not only to the covenant people but to all who would believe.[8] As
Peter wrote, "He [Christ] was destined before the foundation of the
world, but was revealed before the end of the ages for your sake"
(1 Pet 1:20). All people who enter the covenant which God made
through Christ are elected with Christ and incorporated into the
people of God.

Peter wrote this second letter to those who belonged to the people of God. Thus, he speaks a word of encouragement to his readers that if a believer does in fact "confirm" his or her calling and
election, "you will never stumble" (v. 10). This term "stumble" is
normally used to describe sin and sin's consequences.[9] So Peter's affirmation here gives yet another insight into the purpose and effect
on a believer who practices "these things" (v. 8). This is the path to

authentic holiness before God. What he appears to have implied is that an eagerness to "confirm your call and election" (v. 10) is an expression of one's pursuit of God, and thus, holiness.

Peter then adds a marvelous promise to what he has affirmed about the way disciples of Jesus should live. Diligence in actual righteousness and holiness of life is the means by which one finds "entry into the eternal kingdom" (v. 11). Indeed, as Peter wrote elsewhere, "If you invoke as Father the one who judges all people impartially according to their deeds, live in reverent fear during the time of your exile" (1 Peter 1:17). It is our responsibility before God to live in loving obedience in the light of the gospel. There is no contradiction between the grace of God given in Jesus Christ and the holy fear of obedience to the Holy Spirit. God's gift of life makes our obedience possible, but we must yield and choose to follow after the One who chose and pursued us. Indeed, God delights in those who believe him and obey his Word (Zephaniah 3:17)!

The one key which unlocks the secrets of the human heart is the will. As much as God loves humanity and has done to speak to and save human beings, they still retain the ability to say "no" to God. The standard of just judgment by God will be based upon what individuals did with the knowledge that they had of God and of God's saving actions. The Scripture writers are constantly appealing to people to choose based upon their hearing of the Word. The great mystery of how a human being comes to life spiritually and walks into the kingdom should never lead us to deny human choice nor to denigrate the dignity of choice given by God. Whatever one makes of the biblical affirmation regarding predestination, this core teaching about God's gift of genuine human choice must never be compromised.

Three final points are in order to emphasis based on the passage. The first is simply that we who believe have a responsibility to give ourselves completely to the spiritual work of faith. And this work is primarily the moment-by-moment task of striving "to be found by him [God] at peace" (2 Peter 3:14). This remaining at "peace" requires us to choose to remain "in Christ" and to keep to the fellowship of his presence. To do so demands that we learn to practice disciplines of the mind and body, which help us to learn to bring every aspect of our being into conformity with the way of Christ himself.

The second is like the first and is the flip side of our choosing to remain in Christ as he dwells in us by the Spirit. Our choosing to freely submit ourselves allows the Spirit to freely operate with divine power to chisel and shape our character and habits as we obey in faith. The Spirit was given to believers, in part, to form us into the image of the Son of God. This is our destiny. This is why through our participation in the death of Christ, our lives are "hidden with Christ in God" (Colossians 3:3). This is indeed a great mystery, which we are to embrace to give God full room to form us into his glorious children.

The third point is that spiritual work must be expressed in the concrete life contexts and relationships we find ourselves in. And at the core of all relationships is the need to forgive others and show mercy. Indeed, I assert that one of the marks of a person who has forgotten the "cleansing of past sins" (v. 9) is an unwillingness to forgive others. This sin against God and the other person shows a stubborn self-will and effectively stunts all spiritual maturation. All spiritual work is relational, and thus, the love of God has been granted to us to do that work.

CHAPTER 5

Listening to God's Voice
(2 Peter 1:12–19)

"Through the gift of faith we are taught the truth concerning the Son by the Holy Spirit… [T]he Spirit leads us by degrees into the depths, already opened, of the truth of God present within us, and this by explaining, interpreting, incorporating Christ's revealed words in the heart of the believer."[1]

God always speaks to his creatures in one way or another. The question consistently posed in the Word of God is whether we are able or willing to hear the voice of God. The nature and phenomena of created things, the verbal and written testimony of the Scripture, dreams, visions, and wise counsel of other people are ways in which God can and does speak to human beings. Peter here confirms the gospel's testimony that God has spoken supremely and with finality through life and Person of Jesus the Messiah.

Peter sought to "remind you [all] of these things" (v. 12) concerning Jesus Christ and the grace of participation by faith in the kingdom of God. He did this because he knew that his departure from this life was imminent (vv. 13–14). Thus, it was imperative for him to remind the believers of what they already knew about being disciples of the Lord Jesus. God exhorted his people to remember and heed his word repeatedly in the Scripture, and so Peter, the

Lord's servant, did the same by putting in writing this brief summary of teachings on living as God own people.

Are we not blessed, that in the providence of God, Peter made "every effort" to pass on his inspired counsel and warning to the church? Indeed. Hear the apostle's urgent concern: He seeks his readers' attention because he knew that their believing and obeying the Son would be the key to bring them through their life's journey of faith. Not listening is a choice to distance oneself from God and expresses unbelief. Unbelief invites the influence of false teaching.

In every generation and culture in which the gospel has been planted, there are those who level charges of various sorts against the testimony of Scripture to Jesus Christ. In Peter's lifetime, the charge was that the apostles had invented "cleverly devised myths" (v. 16). He counters that with an affirmation of the factual nature of the account about Jesus being transfigured. Contrary to the dismissive charges, they had themselves seen Jesus in God's "glory" and heard God speak of him!

Here's how Luke recorded the event:

> ...Jesus took him Peter and John and James, and went up on the mountain to pray. And while he was praying, the appearance of his face changed, and his clothes became dazzling white. Suddenly they saw two men, Moses and Elijah, talking to him. They appeared in glory and were speaking of his departure, which he was about to accomplish at Jerusalem. Now Peter and his companions were weighed down with sleep; but since they had stayed awake, they saw his glory and the two men who stood with him. Just as they were leaving him, Peter said to Jesus, "Master, it is good for us to be here; let us make three dwellings, one for you, one for Moses, and one for Elijah"—not knowing what he said. While he was saying this, a cloud came and overshadowed them; and they were terrified as they entered the

cloud. Then from the cloud came a voice that said, "This is my Son, my Chosen; listen to him!" When the voice had spoken, Jesus was found alone. And they kept silent and in those days told no one any of these things they had seen. (Luke 9:28–36)[2]

To those of us who have read the New Testament, this account should be familiar. Do we understand it? Christians in these "enlightened" modern times have little appreciation for how extraordinary this account is or why Peter specifically testified to its historical truth. We need to understand why Jesus underwent this "transfiguration," and why God has preserved the account for believers in the Scripture.

First, he reminds his readers that he and the other apostles had "made known to you the power and coming of our Lord Jesus Christ" (v. 16). They had been testifying to the Lord, Jesus of Nazareth, by whom they had directly and personally been trained: He was a flesh and blood person, who did extraordinary acts of healing and deliverance of people from demonic bondage. Jesus the Messiah had expressed his "majesty" (v. 16) throughout his life and ministry, but on the day which Peter references God had confirmed Jesus's identity before the three disciples on the mountain!

Second, Peter recalls the voice and message of "God the Father" to Jesus Christ. The transformation of his appearance and clothing was the outward sign to the disciples' eyes of Jesus's majesty as the only Son of God. The voice of God, "the Majestic Glory," (v. 17) confirmed through the sense of hearing, and upon their minds, his identity as the Son of God and beloved (v. 17). "We ourselves heard this voice come from heaven," Peter affirmed, "while we were with him on the holy mountain" (v. 18).

Peter emphasized the clarity and message of God's voice speaking from the cloud. The other aspects of the event, his appearance, the presence of Moses and Elijah talking to Christ about his mission, and Peter's misplaced suggestion to make shelters for them were apparently less important to him. Why might this be so?

I suggest that the verification of Jesus's identity as the Son and beloved of God is the basis of all the apostolic teaching. If the Lord Jesus was not the beloved Son, then the entirety of the faith crumbles. Thus, Peter cites this account, among the many he could have referenced, when refuting this charge.

God mysteriously revealed the majesty of Jesus Christ the Son—the divine nature and transformed human character—in his body, which was still mortal. The "glory" of Christ's nature as God was expressed so as to become tangible in and through his mortal human body. They perceived this dimly through their senses at the time, but later, the Holy Spirit revealed it more clearly.

Why then did God do this? The account in Mark's gospel makes this clear: "This is my Son, the Beloved; listen to him!" (9:7) Therefore, we must listen to the Son who spoke the truth with his life and words about who God is and what is God's good will for his human creatures. In the eternal Son of God, the Father has spoken with finality about his own holy character and will for human beings who were created in the image of God. All revelation given by the Triune God to human beings is an attempt to communicate his love and goodness and invite them into spiritual relationship in God's life.

The testimony of the apostles is this: God communicated on that extraordinary day by opening the disciples' eyes to see the glory of God in Jesus's mortal body. The majesty expressed his power and the presence of deity. As Peter, James, and John were overwhelmed by the Lord's majesty unveiled before them, so we as readers should be moved to humble silence before our God.

This extraordinary means that God gave to commend his Son to us is not the end. "So we have the prophetic message more fully confirmed" (v. 19.) The Son's life and teaching are a fulfillment of the foreshadowing embedded in what the inspired human authors spoke and wrote in the Scripture. Jesus Christ was the embodied fulfillment of God's promises of Scripture in history.

Thus, believers would "do well to be attentive to this [prophetic testimony] as to a lamp shining in a dark place" (v. 19). For they speak accurately of God's love, will, judgments, and declared plan of action to rescue his creation. That plan of action has Christ as the center and object of human faith in God.

Peter noted in his first letter that the prophets, as they prophesied about salvation to come in Christ, "prophesied of the grace that was to be yours" and inquired of God regarding "the person or time that the Spirit of Christ within them indicated" and they heard the word regarding the "sufferings destined for Christ and the subsequent glory" (1 Peter 1:10–11). The prophetic word spoken and then written was preserved in the Scripture, and this testifies to the ministry, life, death, and resurrection of the Lord Jesus Christ. This is what Peter turned the readers' attention to—lest we forget what God has said to us and how it has been revealed.

According to Peter, Jesus Christ's divine glory and majesty confirm the veracity of the prophetic oracles of Israel's prophets. However, note that he stated they are "more fully confirmed" (v. 19). In addition to the massive amount of material dedicated to addressing God's ancient people in the Scripture, there is also much stated concerning future events that remained unclear for even the most learned biblical interpreters. In linking the "glory" of Christ on the mountain to the "prophetic message," Peter is acknowledging this gap in our grasp of the meaning of Scripture and directing us to center our understanding of that prophetic message around the life and teaching of Jesus Christ. Thus, I think that this is Peter's acknowledgment that we cannot accurately make sense of the Scriptures without reading them through the lens of the teaching and life of Christ himself.

The Lord himself stated, "Do not think that I have come to abolish the Law or the prophets; I have come not to abolish but to fulfill" (Matthew 5:17). And when speaking to prominent religious leaders, "You search the scriptures because you think that in them you have eternal life; and it is they that testify on my behalf. Yet you refuse to come to me to have life" (John 5:39–40). The Scriptures' main object and subject is God himself and his divine activity in the world through the mission of the only Son of God!

The truth revealed in the prophetic writings as well as all portions of Scripture is then like a lamp, illuminating our journey of faith on earth. This is indeed a gift of God to us! So then, until the full dawning of the kingdom becomes reality at our Lord's glorious return, we have the holy Scripture as a source of instruction and encouragement so that we can, by faith, remain steadfast in hope (Romans 15:4). These two testimonies have been united in the biblical texts: The Old Testament witness and apostolic testimony and teaching about Christ are the standard for us—with the life and teaching of Christ in the gospels as the keys to interpreting the whole of the Scripture.

The implications of Peter's testimony are staggering. If a person believes this testimony, their understanding of all of life will be profoundly shaken to the core. The gospel is revolutionary because it affirms that true spiritual power was at home in a human body (that of Jesus of Nazareth). And this good news does not only concern the body of Jesus but also all human beings. For the metaphor of a "tent" is used by Peter to describe our mortal bodies (vv. 12–15). And if we know that Jesus's mortal body (his "tent") was transfigured, then surely, there is hope for those who take refuge in him—not merely for their souls, but their whole persons for eternity![3]

God has come near to us in Christ. In the Lord Jesus, one finds a God who incarnated himself into the form of a human being in order to deliver all who are enslaved to sin and to truly free all who would come to him by faith. And for those who believe and obey the Son, there is hope for becoming victorious over entrenched sinful habits as they learn to be "partakers of the divine nature" (2 Peter 1:4). This occurs as disciples remain with Jesus, "by choice and by grace, learning from him how to live in the Kingdom of God…[That is], how to live within the range of God's effective will, his life flowing through mine."[4]

What then is the right response to such a message? What does the gospel require of those who hear it? To worship God, as revealed in Scripture and Jesus Christ his only Son. To surrender in joyful celebration to the One who is just, pure, full of loving kindness, and exceedingly generous to all his creatures. "All your works shall give thanks to you, O LORD, and all your faithful shall bless you" (Psalm 145:10). And again, "The LORD is faithful in all his words, and gracious in all his deeds" (Psalm 145:15). Thus, we celebrate what God has done through Christ our Lord in the past and in the present.

Yet there are further implications to Peter's affirmations here about the prophetic witness. "You will do well to be attentive to this as to a lamp shining in a dark place, until the day dawns and the morning star rises in your hearts" (v. 19b). Since we know that in Christ we find "confirmation" of the prophetic witness, this then requires us to hold to the remainder of prophesies given. For God will bring the full scope of his promises of judgment and restoration to pass through the ministry of the exalted Lord Christ, for he is the One appointed to bring God's purposes to completion in time and history.

When the Lord returns, he will come as the conquering warrior and judge of Israel's descendants and all peoples of the earth.[5] His first appearance as a humble man in Jesus was to preeminently show the love and mercy of God. His promised return will bring terror to those who do not believe, but for us, this future rule of Christ gives us hope for the future and motivates us to live faithfully now for our Lord.[6]

The confirmation of the promises of the Scriptures in Christ points us toward the future when the fullness of God's rescue plan will be fully enacted. This will be the end of days when God's full restoration work of human lives and of all of creation will become manifested fully. This is the ultimate aim for which we have been saved and which God has chosen us in Christ to forever share in God's divine nature.

CHAPTER 6

Discerning God's Voice
(2 Peter 1:20–2:11a)

"[T]he prophets received their prophecies from God and transmitted what he wanted to say, not what they wanted. They were fully aware that the message had been given to them, and they made no attempt to put their own interpretation on it."[1]

Prophets have been one of the primary ways in which God choose to speak to people in human history. The biblical revelation has in fact come to us through human agents who spoke and/or wrote down God's Word given to them in history by the Holy Spirit. These men and women were God's agents to speak and explain the meaning of his Word and the significance of God's acts in their own time and the future. Thus, it is crucial to keep in mind the means God used to communicate his Word as we try to make sense of how God spoke in the Scriptures and seek to rightly interpret them.

One crucial problem for God's people in ancient times was how to know and how to discern the true voice of God from among the multitude of persons claiming to speak for God. Thus, this practical matter of discerning authentic spokespersons of God is given special attention from Moses before he died, and they go into the land God promised them.[2]

God's ancient people needed practical measures to test who was and was not speaking words from God. Even though today, we have the whole of Scripture available to us, we still need these practical measures. For there are many today who claim to speak for God or to directly know and receive communication from God. And there are many "holy" books which claim to have records of what God spoke in the past through self-proclaimed prophets, and thus, which hold authority over those who believe in them.

The primary mission of the prophet was to speak to the whole people of God concerning God's will for the people of Israel. This means that they rarely spoke words from God to individuals—unless they were in positions of power and influence. The primary prophetic message was to remind the people of God's covenant and confirm the promises and judgments God had laid out in the Torah through the prophet Moses. All prophetic authority in Scripture rests upon the holy work of prophets who communicated the essence of the Torah given through Moses and applied it to all areas of community life. This most often required the prophet to describe how the people and leaders were failing to keep it and what the consequences would be for this.

The prophet thus had a difficult role as the one who communicated God's message to his or her own people. This most often required the prophet to speak against the people and leaders and call out their sins publicly. However, alongside these dire warnings, they also gave encouragement and admonition to stand strong in faith.[3]

The standard test as laid down by Moses is the following: The message spoken in the name of another god other than Yahweh is necessarily false—even if a prediction about something does come to pass; for this is an effort to effectively divert the Israelites attention from the true God to the other "god." If a statement of prediction, given in the name of Yahweh, does not come true then this person is a false prophet and has not genuinely spoken from God.

The core message which the prophet brings must affirm the covenant established by God through the ministry of Moses (Deuteronomy 18:15–19; Isaiah 8:16–20); if this is not central to their message, it does not matter if they can perform miracles or predict the future. Peter knew and assumed the authenticity and authority of prophetic words as recorded in the Scripture. His purpose in this letter is much more specific to the means by which authentic prophetic utterances actually occurred in history through the persons called to prophesy. Peter is asserting both a positive and a negative claim related to this process in order to make a point about the false teachers among the Christian communities.

First of all, he is asserting that the word of prophesy was communicated through specific human beings in specific historical times and places. And when that "word of the Lord"[4] came, it was given in such a way that the messenger could understand it and relay it to others, without changing the meaning or content by applying his or her own interpretation upon it. The human mind of the prophet was fully engaged in hearing and understanding (as much as one could) the content of the message as given by the Holy Spirit while being kept from imposing his or her conceptions upon the message, and thus perverting its content.

Second, Peter asserts that no prophesy ever had its source in the will of a human being. This point is important because it clarifies that the source of prophecy is entirely of God. He demonstrates this by negating the potential of human choice, intelligence, or craft to produce it. The male and female prophets were "moved" or "carried"[5] along by the Holy Spirit to speak exactly what God had told them to say (1:21). This does not mean that they were entirely passive in the process of communicating the Word; rather, their wills and minds were fully engaged in the act of speaking. It seems that Peter's intent here is to emphasize the fact that while the Word was spoken through human agents to other persons, this fact does not necessitate the conclusion that the message had its origins in the mind or the will of the human prophet.

Peter appears to have used the example of the true prophets to combat the influence of the false teachers in churches of his day. For he stated that just as there were "false prophets among" the ancient Israelites, so also there are (and will be) false teachers active in the churches (2:1). Let us heed this so as not to ever become lax in giving due attention to sound doctrine and in testing those who presume to speak and teach the Word in the community of God's people.

In context, Peter is appealing to the Scriptures regarding the true and false prophets. The clearest example of the emergence and influence of false prophets upon God's people is found in Jeremiah.[6] The main charge which God (through Jeremiah) makes against these men is that they were producing what they called the "word of the

Lord" from their own minds. God had never spoken to them nor given them any divine word! The sheer presumption of these men to fabricate a message and peddle it as the word of God to the people of God was an incredibly grave sin indeed.

Peter then described the false teachers who were then active during his own time, describing their tactics, motives, and message. Their methods are inherently deceptive as they use "deceptive words" (v. 3) and means to introduce and teach their "destructive opinions" (v. 1) to believers in the churches. Their motive for taking their message to the churches is greed: They aim to exploit and use the people for their own economic gain and to pull them into their own depraved pursuit of pleasure for its own sake (vv. 2–3; cf. v. 14). Their message appears to fundamentally deny the claims and authority of the Lord Jesus Christ over them (v. 1).

The words Peter uses here tell us several things about these teachers, which are important for understanding why they pose such a grave danger to the community of believers. First is that they have certainly made profession of faith in Christ as Lord and Savior. "They will even deny the Master who bought them" (v. 1). Thus they convince many to listen to them and to adopt their erroneous and destructive opinions about how to live one's life in this world. However, these persons recognize no authority outside themselves, have no fear of God (or the mighty angels); they are bold and stubbornly assert their own will in relation to everyone else (v. 10).

Further, in their practical repudiation of the One whom they called their Master, they are going to bring "swift destruction upon themselves" (v. 1, 4). This just wage for their denial of the Master and for leading others to do the same will surely be exacted on the Day of Judgment by the Lord himself. For they had turned from the way of the Lord to follow their own greed to seek pleasure above all else.[7] These persons are idolaters and do not genuinely follow in the righteous way of Christ. Such persons have a toxic effect upon the community of believers; the assertion of psalmist applies to them:

> The wicked are not so [well planted], but are
> like chaff that the wind drives away. Therefore the

wicked will not stand in the judgment, nor sin-
ners in the congregation of the righteous; for the
Lord watches over the way of the righteous, but
the way of the wicked will perish. (Psalm 1:4–6)

Finally, he asserts that because of these persons and their conduct the "way of truth will be maligned" (v. 2). For nonbelievers will
hear them and conclude that their self-serving and pleasure-focused
way of life is representative of the way of Christ. Thus, the conclusion drawn from their example will be that believers are those who
talk about a Master but who actually serve themselves and seek their
own will and passions.

This should stand as a solemn warning to us about how essential it is for the preachers and teachers of the churches to be practicing obedience to the Lord through faith as they are calling others to
be "obedient to Jesus Christ" (1 Peter 1:2). The conduct of believers
and particularly those who take positions of leadership within the
churches are watched carefully. They become the standard for how
Christian faith is practically defined. Whether we like it or not, this
is a tool of measurement which unbelievers use to gauge and assess
faith in Christ.

The Lord Jesus explicitly warned about the consequences of
denying him before other persons in this life.[8] This example given
by Peter of the repudiation of Christ as Lord carries with it severe
consequences (vv. 4, 9–10; cf. Jude 4). This may strike us as overly
severe, but I would suggest this is because we do not understand the
gravity of this sin. For these persons know the truth about the Lord
and his call to the holy path with him. Knowing the truth, they have
deliberately turned away from the One who is the Truth while speaking of him as Master before other people![9]

The remainder of this passage mostly consists of examples of
God's just punishment for sin in the past. Embedded here is also
an encouraging word about God's preservation of righteous persons
who find that they must live among the wicked. I take this extended
listing as an assurance to believers that God is not unaware of what

wicked persons do and is actively involved with both the righteous and the wicked in this life.

The listing of God's past judgment of his creatures begins with certain angels. Who exactly these "angels"[10] of God are, or when they sinned is not clear from this text. Many biblical interpreters have suggested that they are identical with the "sons of God" mentioned in Genesis just prior to the story of the flood; thus, their grave sin included directly leading to the corruption of human society at that time of ancient history.[11] Regardless of who these beings are, Peter asserted that their punishment of being consigned in chains to "deepest darkness" was both necessary and just (v. 4).

Then he cites the examples of the act of God to destroy human beings in the ancient world by means of the great flood,[12] and the destruction of the cities of Sodom and Gomorrah by reducing them to "ashes."[13] In both cases, these condemnations and specific acts were accompanied by deliverance of small numbers of righteous persons. Notably, Peter asserted that God did this to "make them [inhabitants of Sodom and Gomorrah] an example of what is coming to the ungodly" (v. 6). In the case of the first, the famous example of Noah and his family delivered by the Ark (v. 5) is referenced, and in the second, Noah's relative Lot and portions of his family being led out of the cities before the complete destruction (vv. 7–8).

Notice that this listing is framed in such a way as to communicate the inevitability of God's justice upon wicked persons for their unrighteousness of mind and conduct. The phrases "For if God did not spare" (vv. 4, 5) and "and if" (vv. 6, 7) set up a contrast by which Peter highlighted his conclusion. Namely, that "the Lord knows how to rescue the godly from trial and to keep the unrighteous under punishment until the day of judgment"! (v. 9)

One of the implications of this teaching by Peter, which he draws out later more explicitly in the letter, is that apostolic testimony carries divine authority just as the prophets of God did prior. The New Testament writings are based on the fact that God has given revelation through the declaration of the "word of the Lord" to the Hebrew prophets (as recorded in the Scripture). The Lord Jesus Christ confirmed this, and his apostles reaffirmed it as they were commissioned and empowered by the Holy Spirit to teach all that he commanded. The New Testament writers claim this authority for their testimony of the "Word" as that of the prophetic message of Scripture (2 Peter 3:2).[14]

In the New Testament, we find affirmed (and assumed) the same criteria outlined in passages from the Old Testament scriptures. One finds an emphasis upon looking into the "fruits" of the so-called prophets' life—that the person's life conforms and manifests the goodness of God and character of Christ (Matthew 7:15–23). Any form of "idolatry" is rejected outright, and thus, any speech inspired by idols (gods) is considered to have come from demons and not from God.[15] Any "prophet" must speak the truth according to the standards of the gospel, affirm the incarnation of God in Christ, and must lead people to embrace righteousness of life and not pursue the evil of sin of any kind.[16]

We too can and need to apply these criteria in our day, especially in the context of the exercise of charismatic giftings. Scriptural teaching is that any authentic prophesy given to a believer(s) today for the churches must agree with (and certainly not contradict) God's revealed Word in the Scripture. God's Word never contradicts affirming the goodness of life and relationships, and thus, the primacy of "righteousness" of life for believers is emphatically affirmed as God's good will.

Peter's positive teaching about the means of prophesy communicated and the error of false teachers is a call to be vigilant in seeking to faithfully interpret Scripture with integrity. And in order to do this, we must avoid the evil ways of others who distort the truth for their own gain. One essential means to be able to do this is to recognize and submit to the authority of the Lord Jesus Christ and to Scripture as God's Word and to those duly appointed to serve as leaders in the churches. The outward expression of this submission is obedience to God's Word according to one's knowledge of its teaching. The most effective means to immunize God's people against the influence of false teachers and false teachings is to equip them with clear exposition of the truth from Scripture with exhortation, warning, and vigorous application to righteous action in the whole of life.

CHAPTER 7

Faithfulness among False Teachers (2 Peter 2:11b–22)

"But to comprehend the whole of so great a Subject as this [God's essential nature] is quite impossible and impracticable, not merely to the utterly careless and ignorant, but even to those who are highly exalted, and who love God…seeing that the darkness of this world and the thick covering of the flesh is an obstacle to the full understanding of the truth."[1]

The presence and activity of those who misrepresent the truth in the name of Christ is a common occurrence in every generation of believers. Teachings which either deny or misrepresent the teachings of Scripture and the Lord must be recognized and challenged by the leaders of the Christian community. To ignore this or pretend it could not happen in one's local community is to be willfully blind to the plain testimony of the biblical writers. For plainly "as there were false prophets" in ages past, so now there will be false teachers (2 Peter 2:1).

The various forms that this erroneous teaching takes change from time to time and culture to culture. Sometimes, false teachers are easily recognized due to the theological content of their teaching. But often, they are more difficult to spot because they hide their true motives and purpose. They often do this by hiding behind what appears to be spiritual principles that are broadly in line with Scripture (or at least one can argue that they are in line with it).

The actual focus of these teachers work among the Christian communities is their own self-aggrandizement—to turn the focus, affection, and physical resources of the people toward themselves and their "noble" cause. The aim of false teachers is to take advantage of people and to use and abuse those who follow them. One way or another, at some point or another, their true colors show through because they betray the fact that their goal is to draw people to follow them and not the Lord Jesus Christ.

Peter clearly said that the false teachers he had in mind were motivated by greed and have a completely self-absorbed attentiveness on their own fame. Such persons followed the devil's lead and plunged themselves into the pursuit of gratifying their own evil desires. They do not know and do not listen to the Holy Spirit of God. Instead, they only go after what they imagine to be a spiritual way, which does not impede their pursuit of pleasure.

The Holy Spirit has given us a remarkable gift in leading Peter to write this striking portrait of these teachers. His description of them cuts through the veneer which such persons present in order to deceive others. This section of the letter shows us what to look for in order to spot false teachers when they come into our midst.

The most fundamental point made in this description is that these persons' behavior shows the true source of their supposed "spirituality" and ministry activities. He notes that they have no fear of authority—whether that of angels or among humans—because they presume to possess and wield power over everyone else (vv. 10–11). In asserting such things with such boldness, they show that they have no understanding of spiritual reality! There is no trace of belief in the truth of the gospel or of proper humility before God.

Such persons with characteristic boastfulness, have indeed ceased to be functionally human and have descended to the functional status of mere beasts, which follow only their base instincts (v. 12). Their insatiable pursuit of satisfying their own sinful lusts and impulsive behavior shows that neither conscience nor reason can keep them in check. For they have come to delight entirely in doing their own will and always pursuing self-will, in the pursuit of money, sensual pleasure, and power.

The goal of these teachers is not merely to get things, pleasure, and power for themselves. Rather, they are dead set on enticing as many people as possible to join them in this pursuit (vv. 13–14). The greed they exhibit is shown chiefly in their efforts to control and manipulate other people—and this becomes clear when they are given access to key roles or positions of leadership in the Christian community. They imitate the unclean spirits who animate and prod them on toward the practice of unrighteousness and all forms of wickedness. They actively recruit and attempt to persuade people to leave the "straight road" of Christ's way (v. 15; cf. Matthew 7:13–14) for their love of the wages of sin (vv. 14–15) urges them to bring others onto the wide road, which ultimately leads to destruction.

To illustrate this point, Peter pointed back to Balaam, the false prophet who God prevented from casting a curse upon the nation of Israel.[2] The truth about God's sovereign work for and through Israel was shown to him in a way that he had no choice but to proclaim blessing when asked by Israel's enemies to curse them.[3] He sought to exercise his extraordinary faculties for his own fleshly gain and worldly advancement (vv. 15–16). He used these real abilities to perceive the unseen realms of the world and to take advantage of monetary offers in exchange for cursing others; thus, his actions were for his own gain and not in service to God or the truth. Balaam was capable of speaking the truth—but not because he believed it himself or gladly served the one true God; rather, because God forced him to speak it for the benefit of his own chosen people.

Peter compared these false teachers to this evil man and asserted that they have "left the straight road and gone astray, following the road of Balaam son of Bosor, who loved the wages of doing wrong" (v. 15.) He then goes further and gives us the marks of false teachers, describing them as follows (vv. 17–22): They always promise much but do not deliver anything but empty nonsense about "spiritual freedom," which only enslaves persons. They entice others to join them in their self-indulgence in sensuality (of all different forms). Such persons, while talking a great deal about God and "spirituality,"

are in fact, worldly and mastered by sin. They thoroughly enjoy purs-
ing the lust, which brings corruption to the human person.

Following the example of Balaam, such persons turn away from
the truth of the gospel and actively seek to put stumbling blocks in
the path of those seeking freedom in Christ. The Lord himself states
that some "hold to the teaching of Balaam, who taught Balak to put
a stumbling block before the people of Israel, so that they would eat
food sacrificed to idols and practice fornication" (Revelation 2:14).
For after God strictly prevented Balaam from speaking any word
except blessing upon the Israelites, we read that the men began to
have sexual relations with the women of Moab and to declare loyalty
to their idols (Numbers 25:1–3). Nowhere in the text is the means by
which this happened explained, but when paralleled with the Lord's
words in Revelation, we discover who was behind the plan to put
such opportunities for sin before the ancient Israelites.

These teachers once did possess some knowledge of the truth
about Christ and the gospel, but they departed from truth by choice
and are now entangled in corruption (v. 20). They prove that it is
possible to have some knowledge of God's way of righteousness, salvation, and the practical difference between worldliness and godliness and still choose to be worldly. Such men and women are a warning to us all to avoid the trap of the devil and always pursue Christ
and his way of obedience to the gospel. Further, these teachers know
what they have rejected in order to have now the temporal pleasures
of this brief life. They have chosen that which is merely earthly over
the life that is heavenly. They have turned from reality experienced
in the triune God toward self-absorbed self-worship, which ends only
in death.

The content of the apostles' warning about false teachers sounds
an alarm to believers of their presence in the churches, how they can
be recognized, and why they are so dangerous. What is not addressed
in this letter are the relevant questions related to how believers should
respond to false teachers or prophets when such persons arise. I think
that there are some hints in his words but no direct teaching about
the practicalities of discerning and confronting false teachers. The

following are points which I suggest are implied or are at least consistent with the overall message of this letter.

First is the necessity of taking preventative measures in the lives of believers and in the practical matters of running the local congregation. The primary measure of a spiritually healthy person and congregation is a willingness to listen and obey the gospel and the teaching of the Scriptures.[4] The Lord Jesus spoke of the necessity of diligence for disciples in listening and obeying the truth revealed to them.

> No one after lighting a lamp hides it under a jar, or puts it under a bed, but puts it on a lampstand, so that those who enter may see the light. For nothing is hidden that will not be disclosed, nor is anything secret that will not become known and come to light. *Then pay attention to how you listen; for to those who have, more will be given; and from those who do not have, even what they seem to have will be taken away.* (Luke 8:16–18, italics mine)

The gospel comes to a person, and he or she is faced with a basic decision regarding whether to agree that is it true or not. Full embrace of the gospel is necessary to fully develop spiritually into maturity as an image bearer of God. At the core of true spiritual maturation is transformation. And the core of all spiritual transformation is the engagement of the will to listen and obey the word of God.

Why then does this maturation not happen in some people who do hear the gospel? This can happen when, by choice, a person allows one or all three of the following inner dynamics to work against continued understanding of faith as it is informed by truth from the Scripture: (1) Depending on mere intellectual familiarity with the Bible; (2) giving way to our human tendency to drift away from and not remember basic truths about God and human life; and (3) to consciously attempt to suppress such knowledge of God in order to avoid God's claims as Lord upon us. We, therefore, must listen with careful diligence to Scripture so as to not blunt our spiritual facilities by unbelief and so practice self-deception.

Second is the necessity to "discern the spirits" (see 1 John 4:1–6). While Peter does not make mention of the devil explicitly in this letter, he does warn believers against his evil work elsewhere (1 Peter 5:8–9). Other apostolic writers address the fact that evil spirits animate and empower false teachers. They warn people not to become lax in faith but to choose to discern spiritual truth so they will not be led astray.[5] The only way to avoid this trap of deception is to intentionally seek after the knowledge of the truth for oneself and also to speak and train others to believe and practice it themselves (see 2 Tim 2:14–26). We must immunize ourselves by seeking to walk in the way of Christ (see 2 John 4–6).

We must look very carefully at what a person teaches about the Lord Jesus Christ and his teachings. We must note especially how closely their teaching lines up with the Lord's teaching about himself and his demands. Do they display the righteousness of our Lord, and do they love the people of God? What are their motives for wanting to take such a prominent role in the believing community? "One thing is true. In order to trust fair-seeming people, we should be able to recognize their conduct as simple, steadfast, solid, and well-tried under difficulty, free from affectation, while firm and vigorous in all that is essential."[6]

Those who lead must be open to others examining their lives to verify that they are showing the fruit of righteousness in relationships. To do so is a demonstration of humility, compassion for others, patience, kindness, and other characteristics of our Lord. Arrogance, condescension, or aloofness from others are sure signs of spiritual blindness and a cold heart. The way one lives will show what one believes and whether this matches up to what one teaches. This should be a warning sign to us.

Since our enemy is not our fellow human beings (even if they consider us their enemies), we must learn to engage in spiritual warfare. For we are not merely facing persons but the unclean spirits who are using and abusing these persons to accomplish their evil plans.

Our concern must always be for the persons we are encountering and for working with the Spirit to free them from deception.

Thus, because we are called to "speak the truth" (Eph 4:25) in love to each other, there will come times when direct confrontation with false teachers may be necessary. Since we are to wage war with righteousness, we attempt to persuade them to turn from their error and embrace God's way of righteousness. This must include reproving, rebuking, correcting, and solemnly warning them not to lead others astray (see Titus 1:10–11). But above all, those in positions of leadership must take steps to deprive such persons from access to teaching positions and leadership roles.

False teachers will not remain for long with a community of believers who practice discernment and are alerted to their presence, for they prey on those who are confused, weak, and vulnerable. They are, at heart, cowards and will not stand to be challenged openly unless they believe that they can manipulate enough people to stand with them. It is essential that leaders and people be united in the truth of the gospel in their stand against such persons.[7] In this way, we bear witness and take practical steps to protect the community while leaving such persons to the mercy and judgment of God.[8]

The history of the Christian church gives many examples of leaders using manipulative and forceful techniques in response to heresy and heretics. Political power and the punitive power of government are not effective in turning false teachers away from their errors. Rather, utilizing means of persecution drive them to embrace that erroneous teaching even more tightly (and may make them sympathetic characters to would-be followers). We must follow the example of our Lord Jesus in relation to such persons while seeking to protect God's people from their evil influence.[9]

CHAPTER 8

Waiting for Fulfillment of God's Promises (2 Peter 3:1–10)

"You, O Lord, are my only solace. You, my Father, are eternal. But I am divided between time gone by and time to come, and its course is a mystery to me. My thoughts, the intimate life of my soul, are torn this way and that in the havoc of change. And so it will be until I am purified and melted by the fire of your love and fused into one with you."[1]

The prophetic call to wait with patient faith upon the fulfillment of God's promises redounds throughout the Scripture. God has assured us that there are blessings stored up for those who will wait for the Lord God Almighty to accomplish all that he has said he will do to restore his creation.

> Our soul waits for the LORD; he is our help
> and shield. Our heart is glad in him because we
> trust in his holy name. Let your steadfast love,
> O LORD, be upon us, even as we hope in you."
> (Psalm 33:20–22)

The apostle Peter reaffirms the exhortation to remember God's promises and remain steadfast in faith to the end. Yet he does so with a qualification regarding the source of believers' knowledge of

God's promises: They are to remember the prophetic messages of the prophets as recorded in Scripture and the Lord's command, which have been relayed through the apostles (vv. 1–2). This is crucial because it lays out the authoritative sources which speak to believers as they practice their faith in Christ together. There is a unity among the witnesses of God's spokespersons (prophets and apostles) and this should be the basis of authority for believers.

Peter prophesied for the generations of believers who were to follow him. By the guidance of the Holy Spirit, he warned us of those who stand up to oppose the message of the gospel and mock the testimony of the Scriptures, specifically noting opposition focused on God's acts in creating and intervening in human history. The warning is general (and thus applies generally), but specifically applies to the false teachers whom he referenced earlier in the letter. Just as there will be false teachers in every generation of believers, so also there will be "mockers" of biblical faith.

The focal point of their mockery is the promise of God's future decisive manifestation to human beings to judge persons and nations (v. 4). The manifestation of God's presence or "coming" refers here to God's judgment in the future. In the biblical prophets, this is often referred to as the "Day of the Lord."[2] For example, "Multitudes, multitudes in the valley of decision! For the day of the Lord is near in the valley of decision" (Joel 3:14). This is an assertion personally vouched for by God and repeated throughout the Scriptures and reaffirmed by the Lord Jesus and the apostles.[3]

Whatever else these mockers believe or teach, the one thing they will not accept is that God will actually intervene and act as the judge of human beings! They fundamentally deny and deride others for believing this and also actively try to persuade others to join them in their opinion. They are certain in their own minds that it is a fairy-tale not worthy of human belief.

Further, we are told that these "mockers" are motivated by their own lusts (v. 3). Thus, their objections to the biblical testimony about God and human beings' guilt before God have nothing to do with genuine questions or honest doubts regarding some theological or moral matters. They have already decided to live so as to indulge "their own lusts" (v. 3), and thus, they openly mock biblical faith and deride those who believe.

In order to help believers, Peter lays out a short list of past acts of God in creation and human history and then future acts, which have already been promised. In giving the list, he is giving believers answers by which to reply to mockers of every generation. These are like a guide through both the Old Testament history and the message of the prophets regarding God's actions in the future.

The first charge is that nothing has changed since the days of the ancients, and thus leads to the question of why anyone should take this claim of God's coming to judge the world. Peter answered it (v. 4): He simply asserted that those who make this claim "deliberately ignore this fact, that by the word of God, heavens existed long ago and an earth was formed out of water and by means of water" (v. 5). God's creative act, which formed the heavens and the earth should be enough for those with an open mind to silence this foolish argument.

The power of God which created and formed the world should suffice to establish that—not only does God have the power, but also the right to intervene in his creation. But given that this argument is not accepted, the assertion is pressed forward that by means of water, God also "deluged with water" (v. 6, cf. 2:5) the ancient people of that time so that all died. So then, God's wielding of the same created element to create and to bring his wrath down on the ancient inhabitants of the world should silence them.

If this was not enough reason to listen to God's word given through his chosen messengers, then yet another is added. Peter assured them that the "present heavens and earth have been reserved for fire, being kept until the day of judgment and destruction of the godless" (v. 7). The fact that this world is still here is only because it is being preserved until the time of the final terrible judgment of the wicked. This also means that the present time is the time for people to respond to God's mercy by repentance. In past ages, God was ready and willing to spare righteous persons even in the midst of bringing down his wrath on godless persons.[4] This pattern holds true for the present till that final terrible day when there will be no more hope for human salvation.

Those who condescendingly make fun of biblical teaching and the faith of God's people do so from the conviction that they know better about reality. They have embraced a view of life and the world which excludes God and the claims of God's revelation given in the Scripture. Until this conviction is shaken and they are willing to critically think about whether it is true, then they will be opposed to biblical teaching. Yet God can reach through to such a hardened mind because he is the reality by which we all live. A transformation of intellectually articulated beliefs will only be uprooted in the turning of the human heart, in the recognition of human sin, and complete helplessness before the Creator.

In the modern world, people have deified science and technology. They view the inventions and improvements, which make life on earth easier in many ways, as the mode of salvation. Further, many have rejected faith altogether because they consider "science" to be the ultimate means by which to solve every human problem—not merely the more technical problems related to engineering, making machines, or medical technology for all different purposes. This belief is called "Scientism." Though the numbers of people who wholly devote themselves to it is small, it has held a profound and strong influence on several generations in western countries especially, which are accustomed to industrial development.

Yet long before the astonishing advancements in science and technology people held to the philosophy of "Materialism." This is what the ancient pagans held to in the centuries when the Bible was being written. The pagans mocked the ancient Israelites for their simplistic stupidity of believing in their God. And this contempt was expressed by the Romans among whom the earliest Christian believers lived and gave witness to Christ. In the modern world, there has been an astonishing increase of general knowledge of the world via science and scientific methods of discovering and verifying physical reality. When these are combined with the presupposition that human knowledge and skill is sufficient to control reality, then it becomes plausible for many to think that there is no need for a transcendent God.

Now while Peter is describing the attitudes and actions of those who disbelieve the gospel, he is also addressing believers to help them know how to directly answer these objections. For this ungodly view can be a temptation for those who believe in God—we are not immune from adopting in practice (if not in our stated beliefs) trust in physical resources, human-engineered technology, and powerful persons or institutions to save and preserve our lives.

> The war horse is a vain hope for victory, and
> by its great might it cannot save. (Psalm 33:17)[5]

Like the psalmist, the apostle Peter is warning us to stay clear of the path of those who oppose God's truth, revealed in his written word (Psalm 1). Peter's words here are a prophetic warning to God's people today to learn to trust in God rather than any created thing or their ability to manipulate their circumstances to their desired ends.

Peter now moves to directly address a common problem people have in understanding how to make sense of God's promises. For in terms of how we measure time, and in light of the fact that to us, it has been thousands of years since God declared his promises through the prophets regarding universal restoration, God's actions do seem slow (at best). While God's intervention in history may appear to us as slow or delayed, Peter assured us that this is not the case. The problem lies with us and our perception of God's work in the world.

What some may perceive as slowness to act on God's part is in actuality the manifestation of his patient endurance of human beings in the face of sin. For he has not brought his promises of judgment and full restoration yet in order to give people more time to respond to his merciful invitation to enter the kingdom of God. For God "is patient with you, not wanting any to perish, but all to come to repentance" (2 Peter 3:9). The complaint of God's slowness to act in a final definitive way in human history shows that the persons making it do not really understand what this would mean for them and others. For when the day of God's final reckoning arrives, time will literally come to an end—and with it, the opportunity to exercise faith and be saved.

The time frame for the "day of the Lord" that Peter is referencing is clearly the point when the present creation is destroyed by "fire" (2 Peter 3:10), and all that human beings take for granted about life will disappear. Throughout the Scriptures, the phrase "the day of the Lord" can refer to historical events in which God executes his judgments upon particular nations or cities or peoples. These are points in human history when God intervened or will intervene to accomplish some particular purpose according to his stated will. The apostle Peter appears to be referring to the "day" of final reckoning when wicked persons will have been judged and condemned, and the righteous will be identified and rewarded. On the day, people's eternal destinies will be sealed.[6]

Thus, for the unbeliever, the reality of the Lord's Day will be terror and distress. This is because of their prideful presumption, blindness, and stubbornness against their knowledge of God; for they have the audacity to stand in judgment of God and his ways. For the believer, the Lord's Day can be a source of encouragement during the genuine difficulty of waiting (especially for those suffering) as it brings home the necessity of humility in true faith before God. For both believers and unbelievers, it can be a sign to point towards the reality of God's revelation about his own nature (divine goodness) and wisdom (knowledge which supersedes all) and power (unfathomable).

Contrary to what the false prophets and teachers of our day proclaim, the future does not bode well for most people for they no longer believe in a God who holds anyone ultimately accountable or punishes people for their sin. To affirm this is now considered heresy! But God's people must stand firm in the testimony of the Scriptures for God is the sovereign and the righteous judge. To believe in the gospel is to believe in God as the judge and king of the earth he created.

Then shall all the trees of the forest sing
for joy before the LORD; for he is coming, for he

is coming to judge the earth. He will judge the
world with righteousness, and the peoples with
his truth. (Psalm 96:12–13)

The apostles affirmed both the just judgments of God and the
extravagant grace of God to human beings. We must hold to them
both and learn to live in "reverent fear" of God (1 Peter 1:17) during
our time on earth. We must also not shrink back from proclaiming
to people what the alternative to faith will ultimately bring upon
them—condemnation and eternal separation from God.[7] And we
must not withhold from anyone the extraordinary promise of life
eternal for all who will embrace the Lord Jesus and enter the kingdom of God through him.[8]

If we desire to mature in faith by learning to wait for God to
act at the appointed time, then we must bring our thinking into line
with the Word. This means we must disregard how nonbelievers view
time and reality. Peter helps us by reaffirming the metaphor of God's
perspective on time, which Moses proclaimed (Psalm 90:4): A day
on earth is like a thousand years and a thousand years is like one day
to God (2 Peter 3:8). What we call a short or long period of time is
neither short nor long to God. God measures the timing of events by
a different means and he acts with eternity in mind.

We perceive everything through the narrow "lenses" of our
minds because we inhabit what we call "time." Like fish who only
know what it is like to swim in water, we perceive reality from within
time. It is true that God is present in time as God is present everywhere; however, he lives in his own eternity and is never bound as we
are by time.

As the eternal God, he is the One who created and fashioned
the heavens and earth—and in doing so, he created what we call
"time." God intervenes and acts in time and history, and this is what
we can know through what Scripture records, or what we directly
experience as the kingdom is manifested. But we do not perceive
God's actions from God's perspective. Thus, we confuse what we see
with God's being "slow" to act.

Peter reminds us of God's extraordinary patience and long suffering with us. This is one more way that God shows his grace to believers. Since this is the case, we need to remember to be gracious to those who mock our faith or oppose the gospel for we know that God desires for all people to come to repentance and receive salvation in the Lord Jesus Christ (3:9). To affirm God's grace is as necessary as believing in God's ultimate judgment on the day of God. The reason we have been called to bear witness to others is precisely because of the reality of judgment and salvation.

CHAPTER 9

Necessity of Ardently Seeking God (2 Peter 3:11–18)

"To know God is at once the easiest and the most difficult thing in the world. It is easy because the knowledge is not won by hard mental toil, but is something freely given. As sunlight falls free on the open field, so the knowledge of the holy God is a free gift to men who are open to receive it. But this knowledge is difficult because there are conditions to be met and the obstinate nature of fallen man does not take kindly to them."[1]

The apostle Peter explicitly confirms what the prophets said in the Scriptures: The day of God's judgment upon all the people who have lived on earth is assured and just. The natural world will one day be "dissolved with fire."[2] Thus all that wicked people hold onto and make idols of will cease to exist. Only those who act on faith in Christ will survive and enjoy the "new heavens and a new earth."[3] The hope of salvation found only in Christ is grounded in the fact that the physical world God created will not endure forever and that God will renew all his creation.

Therefore, God's promises point beyond this presently created order, which has embedded within it corrupting elements that ensure its ultimate extinction. Faith sees beyond this world to the beauty and permanence of the new creation which God has promised to make after all his decrees have been enacted related to human destinies.[4] This entirely new order of creation will be the true home for redeemed humanity (v. 13).

These facts should drive us to sober judgment about ourselves and how we live our lives now. This assertion, conveying the truth stated in Scripture, was a refutation of the common notions among pagan people in the lifetime of Peter that the physical world would exist perpetually much as it did then (see 2 Peter 3:4). This will not be so! And thus, since God will melt everything down by fire in the future, believers must now lead "lives of holiness and godliness" (v. 11).

Peter emphasized the connection for believers of actively expecting God's intervention to end the created order with the ardent practice of holiness and godliness. His exhortation is direct: What sort of people ought you and I to be? (v. 11) The obvious answer is supplied, and it sharply contrasts with "the corruption that is in the world because of [human] lust" and degrading behavior that we all observe in ourselves and others (see 2 Peter 1:4). We who belong to God and to Jesus Christ must live upright lives before the watching eyes of unbelievers—regardless of how much this will cost us. This conduct of life is a sign of the hope we have in the Lord.

There is an additional and unexpected insight given here by Peter regarding the effects of and the possible motivation for our "leading lives of holiness and godliness" (v. 11). That is, in following ardently after our Lord in God's appointed way, we show that we are waiting for and hastening the "coming day of God" (v. 12). What does this mean? His point here seems to be that our practice of faith somehow activates and facilitates the Holy Spirit's work in the lives of others.

In a faithful response to God's grace, we are modeling and being God's catalysts for the gospel through actively serving God while waiting by faith for the Lord's return. The fuller God's people are given over to the work of the kingdom, the greater will be the manifestation of God's power on earth. The faithful witness and service of God's people in their own time effects change in culture and society. The ministry of redeemed humans on earth now is empowered and carried along with the power of God's kingdom so that believers actively "lead lives of holiness and godliness" (v. 12). This manner of life shows its full measure when we express boldness that comes from love. And in the practice of God's love, we become, in some measure, as the risen Christ is now, as we live in this world.[5]

When God's people on earth faithfully serve the Master, then God's purpose of spreading his word of truth far and wide is advanced. And when everyone has heard the gospel and thus has an opportunity to repent and believe, then the day of our Lord's return as judge will come.[6] This was part of the message of Peter preached to the large crowd in Jerusalem that they needed to repent "so that your sins may be wiped out, so that times of refreshing may come from the presence of the Lord, and that he may send the Messiah appointed for you, that is, Jesus, who must remain in heaven until the time of universal restoration that God announced long ago through his holy prophets" (Acts 3:19–21). There will a completely new start with new pure creation and with redeemed and pure human beings inhabiting it.

The apparent "delay" in the Lord's promised return to rule on earth and remake heaven and earth is a mercy that should cause one to fear God. God is showing mercy to wait and give you and I (and others) opportunity to repent and be reconciled. For God will not be responsible for anyone perishing (2 Peter 3:9)! God's patience and kindness are given so as to lead us to repentance and find eternal life (Romans 2:4; John 3:16–17). This warning about the eventual destruction of all created matter in the universe and promise of God creating a new "heaven" and new "earth" give us all a warning long before this happens.

For the biblical writers, theological teaching that is grounded in revelation should inform how we live our lives now. Thus, Peter exhorts his readers to actively and persistently "strive" (v. 14)[7], with all their energy, toward the practice of holiness and be devoted to God in every aspect of life. Earlier in the letter (1:16–18), he had specifically cited the fact that Jesus had been transfigured—showing evidence of the fullness of the kingdom of God being briefly manifested in his physical body.[8] At the end of the letter, he appears to be appealing to revelation again; but here, toward the time when God's kingdom will fully reign and inhabit the created order. Then the Lord—who is "our righteousness"[9]—will be able to make himself at home in his own creation forever.

The Holy Spirit gives spiritual confirmation of the certainty of the kingdom of God to come in the future—in full form, with the manifestation of goodness in human lives. This blessed hope gives a sound motive for believers to maintain peace with God and is yet one more reason for believers to seek God's kingdom now (Matthew 6:33): To consciously avoid choosing to assert self-will (1 John 2:29–3:3), to turn from knowingly resisting the voice of the Holy Spirit (Hebrews 3:12–14), and to quickly come to God in confession of sin for cleansing in the blood of Christ (1 John 1:8–2:2). The fact that everything is to be exposed to God's "fire" means that everything people do in the body will not survive unless done out of genuine faith—all clinging to anything of this earth and deeds done for self-aggrandizement will be lost.[10]

The apostle desires for his readers to accurately understand how to live out the gospel. So he makes specific exhortations to further clarify what the right response to God is in light of the certain end of the world. First, they are to "make every effort to be found by him at peace, without spot or blemish" (v. 14). Second, while they remain at peace with God, they should take upon themselves the truth that God's patience is extended for the sake of salvation (v. 15).

The first exhortation echoes back to what he had begun his letter asserting the need for doing what is right in relationship with God and others while aiming for specific moral formation of one's character. This is done through disciplines, which set oneself apart for God; these open oneself up for the transformation of one's character to be like that of Christ himself (see 1:5–8). But how are these practices related to being "found by him at peace"? Simply put, these are the concrete actions which we must take continually to stay on the road, walking with our Lord and God and carrying his yoke (Matthew 11:28–30).

To practice righteousness is the only way to avoid wandering off from God's purpose for our lives. The distractions around us are too numerous, and the influence of our inclinations and habits often still have the scent and form of sinful behavior. The moral stench of the false teachers (2:13) is a striking reminder to believers of the ruin individuals or groupings of people can make of God's gifts in this life. To try to remain still and stagnate in our practice of faith is evidence of already desiring to wander off the straight road. Thus, we are to walk forward with God, continually practicing faith and so be at peace with God.

The second exhortation is a phrase concisely summarizing the call to faith he made in relation to the objections of those who make fun of believers (3:3–4). The fact that we must wait for Lord Jesus's promised return to earth shows that God is patient! And because he is patient, this means that salvation remains available to those who have not yet believed. For truly God desires for no person to perish and thus neither should we! Thus, a mature view of the need to wait for the Lord's return is to see more opportunities to share the incredible Good News of our Lord with those around us.

Peter then wrote something that is a bit surprising (at least to me). He mentioned the apostle Paul and some of his writings, which his readers had also received and become familiar with. These comments are very instructive for several reasons. One is that this is one of the rare instances in the apostolic letters where an apostle mentions a fellow apostle by name with explicit reference to his writings. Two is that Peter clarified the truth in regard to the specific content of Paul's writings in order to refute the false teachers he has denounced in his own letter. Three is that there is a basic principle of biblical interpretation embedded into these comments. Let us carefully look at and glean from this precious passage truths, which we can put into practice.

In the New Testament, references by apostles to other apostles are rare.[11] In the case of Peter and Paul, we know much more about their interactions because of Paul's letter to the Galatians. There, Paul affirmed the apostolic ministry of Peter and asserted that Peter (with the apostles and other leaders) had affirmed his apostolic ministry.[12]

Peter assumes the legitimacy of Paul's ministry by citing Paul's letters as bearing the marks of divine wisdom, having apostolic authority, and thus being part of the whole of holy Scripture (vv. 15–16).[13] These assertions about Paul's letters are embedded in his refutation of these teachers' perversion of Paul's intended meaning. For these teachers had apparently taken and lifted out of their context certain phrases from Paul's letters[14] and misused them to convince people that their teaching agreed with Paul's (or perhaps that Paul taught the same things as they did)—thus giving it legitimacy before others. However, Peter reminded us that these claims were based upon their selectively twisted or "tortured"[15] misuse of the content of Paul's letters. They were attempting to force Paul's words so they would appear to agree with their own perverse ideas. Such persons "twist [Paul's writings] to their own destruction, as they do to the other scriptures" (v. 16).

The content of Paul's letters bore witness to the same point Peter had labored to make for his readers. Namely, that God's patience is an expression of his kindness and his desire for all people to come to repentance and thus find eternal salvation.[16] This is the main point Peter made through this last portion of his short letter. The false teachers have taken advantage of the fact that there are some portions of Paul's letters which are "hard to understand" and thus, easier to intentionally "twist" their true meaning (v. 16). This strategy comes from the demons as they imitate their master Satan, who used Scripture to tempt Jesus to step off the road set before him into ministry and self-sacrifice on our behalf (Matthew 4:6).

The biblical principle embedded in Peter's statement regarding Paul's letters is the following: That the authors of Scripture were given wisdom and insight rooted in revelation. Revelation of truth, as a matter of course, cannot be understood rightly by those who have not been born anew in the Holy Spirit.[17] Such persons are "ignorant" and spiritually "unstable" because they do not know God through the Lord Jesus Christ.[18] Men and women like this may be very intelligent, highly educated, and gifted leaders. However, because they remain spiritually blind, they cannot but do violence to the meaning of Scripture if they try to teach and interpret it for others.

Finally, Peter concludes his letter by reiterating what he had already taught in some detail (vv. 17–18). In these last sentences, he sums up with brevity the core teaching he wants his readers to remember and put into practice. Specifically, reaffirming the warning given about following false teachers, exhorting all to be on guard to avoid error, and above all else, pursue God.

This exhortation is on the one hand negative and on the other positive. This is important because we are always faced with choices in which we must say no to something and then yes to something else. When we are confronted with false teachers and their erroneous teachings that pervert the gospel, we must say no to their appeal. And we must reaffirm being Jesus's disciples moment by moment and day by day as we listen to hear his voice alone.

The false teachers, whether those in Peter's time or our own, make an appeal to us to join them. But for us to do that means forsaking our Lord and embracing an error taught by persons who are "lawless." This term is used by Jesus and the apostles to describe people who have chosen to abandon the truth because they think that they are above all authority in regard to spiritual things.[19] If anyone turns away from the truth of the gospel to follow such persons, they will "lose" their spiritual "stability" (v. 17), which comes from knowing the One God in truth through the Son, according to the Scriptures.

In order to avoid the ruin of our lives for eternity, we must turn and pursue God by opening ourselves fully to grow up into the "grace and knowledge of our Lord and Savior Jesus Christ" (v. 18). Knowing him is the foundation of life. He is the solid rock upon which to build up our faith and continually rise up into knowledge of God. In order to continually grow up into grace and knowledge of God, it is necessary to reverently hear and study the Word of God written (the Scriptures) and do everything we can to learn how to properly understand and interpret the scriptures in their context, with hearts set upon obeying our faithful God.

We must never substitute our own ideas for or in place of what Scripture clearly teaches. And we must be open to be corrected by the plain teachings of the Scripture—even as Peter was open to hear God's wisdom regarding salvation in the writings of Paul. And following the example of Peter, we need to be open to hearing God's corrective word to us through our brothers and sisters. For Peter heeded Paul's rebuke (see Galatians 2:11–14) and humbly recognized that Paul had been gifted to teach divine wisdom about God's salvation in Christ (v. 15). May God grant us ears to hear as the blessed Spirit of Jesus speaks to his people.

Afterword

One of the primary purposes of 2 Peter is to hold out an invitation. The apostle Peter made this invitation on behalf of the Lord Jesus to all who would read these words in faith. He longed, with sanctified desire, for his hearers to receive spiritual life and so experience the great joy of obedience to God in light of his "great and precious promises," confirmed in Messiah Jesus. Thus, we find an emphasis throughout this brief letter on putting faith into action.

The apostle Peter's design was to remind them of the basic framework of the faith so that they would remain established together in the practice of the faith. In this way, they could put into practice these teachings and have an "antidote" to the influence of false teachers and "the world." This much seems clear enough from a careful reading of the letter of 2 Peter.

Yet there is a primary question not directly answered in 2 Peter: How do I (we) put his instructions into practice? This question is quite reasonable since he began the letter by exhorting us to "add to" our faith by learning to practice certain virtues (see 1:5–11) and to heed the revelation God has given in the Person of the Lord Jesus Christ. Then after warning of the dangerous influence of these teachers to the churches and answering the mockers of the faith, he concludes with another exhortation to grow up into "the grace and knowledge of our Lord and Savior Jesus Christ" (3:18).

This question of how to implement the truth expounded by the apostle Peter is crucial for several reasons. This must be answered in the most practical and concrete ways for truth to work through me and effect lasting change within me. I write this with special urgency as one who teaches and leads others in Christian communities. How urgent it is for us, believers, to counter the human and thoroughly modern tendency to erect walls between what is true and what is real. We must push back against every stronghold with the spiritual weapons of God, perpetually yielding to the Holy Spirit every creative and intelligent faculty gifted to us by God. To do so marks the path of freedom for leaders, teachers, and all other believers.

In order to be equipped to lead by example and speak and teach accurately from Scripture about the Lord's way of life for his disciples, we must all first learn to practice the truth of the gospel with a whole, undivided heart. For who in their right minds would dare to venture out to lead others without first knowing the terrain of the path they expect others to follow? (Unfortunately, many do.) May God heal and raise up leaders of his people who continually submit to God and learn his way before presuming to teach others!

Part of the answer is captured by Henry Scougal:

> But now, that I may detain you no longer, if we desire to have our souls moulded to this holy frame, to become partakers of the divine nature and have Christ formed in our hearts, we must seriously resolve and carefully endeavor to avoid and abandon all vicious and sinful practices. There can be no treaty of peace till once we lay down these weapons of rebellion wherewith we fight against heaven; nor can we expect to have our distempers cured if we be daily feeding on poison. Every wilful sin gives a mortal wound to the soul and put it at a greater distance from God and goodness; and we can never hope to have our hearts purified from corrupt affections unless we cleanse our hands from vicious actions.[1]

Another part of the answer to this question of practical implementation is that we learn to pray. The practice of prayer in the midst of the concrete circumstances of our lives is the means and classroom of the Holy Spirit appointed for the Lord's disciples. Peter emphasizes the importance of prayer in the letter of 1 Peter (see 1 Peter 3:7; 4:7; 5:6–8).

The practice of faith and prayer are mirror images of each other. For true faith is essentially relational, and it requires us to perpetually receive the grace and mercy of God by opening ourselves to knowing the Truth himself. A merely humanly devised intellectual system of thought, even if it accurately reflects the teaching of Scripture to a large extent, is little more than an outward shell with nothing inside. It is a representation of God's truth without the corresponding reality of God's presence and power active in the hearts and minds of persons in community.

Mere devotion to religious rituals or communities of faith—even for those who base their teachings on the Scripture—is not enough to give one right-standing relationship with God. Such relationship is found only through the person of the Lord Jesus Christ and by openness to the Holy Spirit, who reveals God's character by dynamically illuminating Christ's life and teaching. To receive such knowledge requires one to yield to Christ as Master and to obey Him as an apprentice in the way of the gospel in a specific community of believers. And God always leads his beloved ones into experiential knowledge of himself and his ways—primarily as they learn together to pray.

The hope granted us in our Lord Jesus comes wholly from God, who is the Truth and is faithful to his promises. We need only to entrust ourselves to the Father and repent of our foolish vanity and unbelieving pride.

"Humble yourselves therefore under the mighty hand of God, so that he may exalt you in due time. Cast all your anxiety on him, because he cares for you." (1 Peter 5:6–7)

To say that we cannot learn to walk in God's ways is an affront to the Majesty above, whose word is true and who has assured us of his very own power to lead "lives of holiness and godliness, waiting for and hastening the coming of the day of God" (3:11–12).

Henry Scougal addresses this point well:

> Now, in this case, we cannot excuse our-
> selves by the pretence of impossibility, for sure
> our outward man is some way in our power; we
> have some command of our feet, and hands,
> and tongue, nay, and of our thoughts and fan-
> cies too, at least so far as to divert them from
> impure and sinful objects and to turn our mind
> another way; and we should find this power and
> authority much strengthened and advanced,
> if we were careful to manage and exercise it. In
> the meanwhile, I acknowledge our corruptions
> are so strong and our temptations so many that
> it will require a great deal of steadfastness and
> resolution, of watchfulness and care, to preserve
> ourselves even in this degree of innocence and
> purity.[2]

The trouble most of us seem to have is that the scope and power declared in God's promises seem unreal to us. And since our experience tends to not line up with the stupendous claims of God in the Scripture, many of us decide that a kind of practical atheism makes more sense. Is this not part of why God revealed his word through his promises? Our practical atheism must be exposed so we can choose to renounce that and fully and unreservedly open ourselves to the Holy Spirit. To retain this practical atheism is to push away the truth of God's promises through unbelief and thus grieve the Holy Spirit. Our actions will demonstrate what we actually believe.

The grace of God granted to those who long to learn to pray is an expanded heart and open mind, an increasing willingness to listen, and the corresponding ability to hear the truth as God communicates to us. The particular forms which prayer may take are less important than praying from one's heart by faith in response to the truth of God's promises. God delights in such persons and takes joy in dwelling within them—revealing his love and truth to and through them.

"There is no reason to marvel at God's granting such subline and strange gifts to souls he decides to favor. If we consider that he is God and that he bestows them as God, with infinite love and goodness, it does not seem unreasonable. For he declared that the Father, the Son, and the Holy Spirit would take up their abode in those who love him by making them live the life of God and dwell in the Father, the Son, and the Holy Spirit [Jn. 14:23]."[3]

The apostle Peter's exhortation was to open our hearts to the provision of God already gifted to us through "knowledge of him who called us by his own glory and virtue" (1:3). And as we cultivate within ourselves practices that will foster genuine openness to God, the Spirit changes our capacity to receive his "precious and very great promises" (1:4). Thus, in so doing, we can say no to the corrupting alure of lust because by faith, we live as "partakers of the divine nature" (1:4, RSV).

Prayer is the act by which faith is stimulated and strengthened in light of God's promises as the Lord Jesus manifests his power in those trusting in him. Thus we are exhorted in the Scriptures to entrust ourselves to the living God and learn to be obedient children in all things. This is the invitation of the Holy Spirit to us all. Let us receive the grace of God and diligently walk the path of living God's life together.

Endnotes

Chapter 1

1 Andrew Murry, *Abide in Christ*, from *The Andrew Murray Collection* (Barbour Books), p. 100 (italics in original).
2 A common description of Jesus by other leaders in the New Testament was the "Righteous One" (see Acts 7:52; 22:14; cf. Hebrews 1:9; 1 John 2:1–2).
3 "Righteousness," *Dictionary of the Later New Testament & Its Developments* (IVP), p. 1054.
4 See 1 Peter 1:18–21; 1 John 2:1–2; 1 Timothy 2:5; Hebrews 10:19–25.
5 cf. Acts 2:32–35; 10:42–43; 1 Peter 3:22.
6 cf. Genesis 1:1; Psalm 148; Isaiah 40:25–28; John 1:1–4; Revelation 4:11.
7 Matthew 6:32–33; cited from God's New Covenant: A New Testament Translation, Cassirer (Eerdmans, 1989).
8 cf. Exodus 24:15–18; 34:5–8; 2 Chronicles 7:1–3; Psalm 96; Isaiah 6:1–4; John 12:23–28; 1 Peter 1:21; 4:12–16.
9 "Glory," New Bible Dictionary, 3rd ed. (IVP), p. 414.
10 "Glory," *Dictionary of Jesus and the Gospels* (IVP), p. 269.
11 cf. Deuteronomy 7:6–11; Psalm 138:1–3; Isaiah 43:4–7; John 17:1–5.
12 cf. Exodus 20:1–17; Deuteronomy 7:7–11; Isaiah 44:1–8; Revelation 5:11–14.
13 cf. John 6:25–58; 7:37–39; 15:5; 1 Corinthians 12:12–13; Ephesians 1:22–23.

Chapter 2

1 Venerable Bede, cited from Ancient Christian Commentary on Scripture, vol. 11, ed. Gerald Bray (IVP, 2000), p. 133.
2 This teaching is given in slightly different ways elsewhere; see 1 Peter 2:1–3; 1 Corinthians 6:9–20; Colossians 3:1–4.
3 cf. Exodus 20:17; Matthew 23:25; Luke 12:15; 16:13; Colossians 3:5; James 3:13–4:4; 2 Peter 2:3, 14.
4 cf. Exodus 12:28–39; 14–15; Psalm 106; Isaiah 43:1–13; Matthew 6:13.
5 cf. Luke 10:21–22; John 2:11, 13:12–17, 14:5–14, 17:1–4.

Chapter 3

1 St. Basil, On the Spirit, chap. 1, para. 2, cited from The Nicene and Post-Nicene Fathers, 2nd series (T & T Clark/Eerdmans, 1996), p. 2.

2 cf. 1 Peter 1:22–2:4; 1 John 2:15–17.

3 cf. Hebrews 5:11–14.

4 cf. James 2:14–26; 2 Timothy 1:7.

5 1 Peter 1:13–15; 2:4–5, 11–12; cf. Hebrews 11:23, 12:7–13.

6 This Greek word *arête* is elsewhere used to describe the manifestation of God's power ("mighty deeds" [1 Peter 2:9] and "excellence [manifests power]." See *A Greek-English Lexicon of the New Testament and Other Early Christian Literature* (BDAG), 3rd ed., Walter Bauer, rev. and ed. Frederick William Danker (University of Chicago Press, 2000), p. 130.

7 *New Bible Dictionary*, p. 424.

8 Exodus 33:17–23, 34:5–10; Psalm 25:6–15; Mark 10:18; Titus 3:4.

9 cf. Matthew 12:35; Romans 16:19; Hebrews 10:23–25; 3 John 11.

10 cf. Psalm 119:63–68; Proverbs 1:7; 8:8–14. "The apostles stressed the necessity for those who know God to live a godly life (1 John 2:3–4; 5:18) and that Christ taught them the will of the Father." (*The Expositor's Bible Commentary*, vol. 12, p. 269).

11 cf. Jeremiah 22:13–17; Micah 6:8; Matthew 11:27; John 15:12–17.

12 The Greek word here is *egkpateia* (see BDAG, p. 274).

13 cf. Isaiah 26:7–9, Psalm 63, Proverbs 28:5.

14 cf. Mark 8:34–38; 2 Peter 3:17; Zephaniah 2:3.

15 The Greek word used is *hupomonen*: "the capacity to hold out or bear up in the face of difficulty, *patience, endurance, fortitude, steadfastness, perseverance*" (BDAG, emphasis in original, p. 1039).

16 cf. Psalm 138:1–3; Luke 8:15; Romans 5:3; James 1:2–4; 1 Peter 2:18–21.

17 See Hebrews 2:17–18, 4:14–16, 5:5–10.

18 See 2 Peter 2:9; 3:11. The Greek word here *eusebeian* carries the sense of "awesome respect accorded to God, *devoutness, piety, godliness*." (BDAG, emphasis in original, 412.)

19 *New Bible Dictionary*, p. 422; cf. Exodus 20:1.

20 cf. Luke 2:25, 4:1–13; Hebrews 5:7; Isaiah 11:2–3. In the Scripture, Enoch (Genesis 5:24) and believers in general (Hebrews 12:28–29) are given as examples.

21 cf. 1 Peter 1:22, 3:8; Romans 12:10; 1 Thessalonians 4:9; Hebrews 13:1. The Greek word here, *philadelfian*, is a compound word that combines "love" (*phileo*) and "brothers" (*adelphoi*); thus, it is often translated as "brotherly kindness" (see KJV, NKJV, NASB, NIV). The term carries sense of having mutual affection, special concern or interest, and love among associates or friends (see *BDAG*, pp. 1055, 1056).

22 Leviticus 19:17–18; Psalm 133; 1 Peter 1:22; 1 John 4:19–21.

23 cf. Luke 7:34; John 11:3; Revelation 3:19; Hebrews 2:10–18.

24 The Greek word used here is *agapen*; the sense it carries is "the quality of warm regard for and interest in another, *esteem, affection, regard, love* [but this not limited to intimate relationships]." (*BDAG*, emphasis in original, p. 6.)

25 cf. Deuteronomy 7:6–11; Isaiah 49:15; 66:13; Hosea 11:1–4.

26 cf. Deuteronomy 6:5, Psalm 116, Joshua 22:5; see *New Bible Dictionary*, pp. 700–702.

27 cf. John 13:34–35; Matthew 5:48; Luke 6:27; 1 John 4:7–21.

28 cf. Matthew 25:31–46, Luke 10:29–37, Ephesians 5:1–3, James 2:14–17.

29 E. M. Bounds, *The Necessity of Prayer*, cited from *The Complete Works of E. M. Bounds on Prayer* (Baker, 2004), p. 14.

Chapter 4

1 A. W. Tozer, The Root of the Righteous, quote from essay titled "About Hindrances," pp. 130–1.

2 See also Deuteronomy 6:1–15, 8:18; 1 Chronicles 16:7–36; Psalm 111; Isaiah 46:3–13.

3 John 9; 10:24–28.

4 See also Psalm 119:73–80, Matthew 7:21–23, Romans 6:1–4ff., James 2:18–26.

5 See Genesis 12:1–3; 13:14–17; 15:5–21; 17:9–14, 17–21; 22:15–18; 26:2–5; 28:13–15; 35:9–12.

6 See Deuteronomy chapters 27–30.

7 Deuteronomy 29:29; Ephesians 3:8–11; 1 Peter 1:10–12.

8 Acts 1:8, 11:15–18; Ephesians 2:11–20, 1:17–21.

9 See Psalms 37:24, 119:65; Proverbs 3:23; Hosea 14:8–9; Malachi 2:8; John 11:9; 1 Peter 2:8.

Chapter 5

1 Prayer, Hans Urs Von Balthasar, trans. A. V. Littledale (Sheed & Ward, 1961), p. 58.

2 See parallel passages in Matthew 17:1–9 and Mark 9:2–10.

3 See 1 Peter 1:21; 1 John 3:1–3; 1 Corinthians 15:21–23; 2 Corinthians 5:1–5.

4 Dallas Willard, *The Divine Conspiracy* (San Francisco: HarperCollins, 1998), p. 283.

5 See Exodus 15:3, Psalm 96:10–13, Mark 13:24–27, Matthew 26:64, John 5:25–29, Revelation 19:11–16.

6 See 2 Peter 3:11–14; 1 Thessalonians 5:1–11; Isaiah 33:20–22.

Chapter 6

1. Oecumenius, Commentary on 2 Peter; quoted from Ancient Christian Commentary on Scripture NT, vol. 11, gen. ed. Thomas Oden (IVP, 2000), p. 141.
2. See Deuteronomy 13; 18:15–22.
3. For example, predictions of certain destruction and loss to the nation of Israel (Deuteronomy 28; Isaiah 24:1–23; Jeremiah 6:16–26; Ezekiel 13:8–16, 20:33–39) and messages of salvation and restoration (Deuteronomy 30:1–5; Isaiah 12:1–6, 49:5–6, 62:1–12; Lamentations 3:22–33; Zechariah 9:11–12, 16–17).
4. This phrase is used frequently in the writings of the prophets to introduce the source of the messages they received from God to speak to their contemporaries.
5. This is the primary meaning of the Greek term that Peter uses here. (See *BDAG*, p. 1051.)
6. See Jeremiah 5:7–15, 14:13–16, 23:23–32.
7. See also Paul's comment that greed is an expression of "idolatry" (Colossians 3:5). Tellingly he then adds, "On account of these the wrath of God is coming on those who are disobedient."
8. See Matthew 10:32–33, Luke 12:8–9.
9. See Matthew 7:21–23; 2 Timothy 2:11–13; Titus 1:13–16.
10. The Greek term is best translated literally as "messengers."
11. See Genesis 6:1–5.
12. Genesis 6:5ff.
13. 2 Peter 2:6; cf. Genesis 19:24–29.
14. See 2 Peter 3:2; Ephesians 2:20; the New Testament writers take for granted that the prophetic writings have equal weight of divine authority as God's word along with their own teaching.
15. See 1 Corinthians 12:1–3, Acts 16:16–18.
16. 1 John 2:18–27; 2 John 7–10; Revelation 2:20–23.

Chapter 7

1. Gregory Nazianzen, 2nd Theological Oration, chap. 4, cited from The Nicene and Post-Nicene Fathers, 2nd series, vol. 7 (T&T Clark/Eerdmans: reprint 1996), p. 290.
2. The full story of Balaam is recorded in Numbers 22–24.
3. See Numbers 22:20, 35, 38; 23:3, 12, 16, 26; 24:2, 12–13; Deuteronomy 23:4–5.
4. See 2 Peter 1:19; 3:17–18.
5. For example, 2 Corinthians 11:1–4; 1 Timothy 1:3–7; 6:3–12; 2 Timothy 3:1–17; Hebrews 13:1–16.

6   Fenelon, *The Royal Way of the Cross*, ed. Hal M. Helms (Paraclete Press, 1982), p. 73.

7   See Romans 16:17–20; 1 John 2:18–25; 2 John 7–11; 3 John 5–12.

8   The most detailed directions of practical steps to take in response to false teachers is concisely summarized in Jude 17–23.

9   For a concise scholarly treatment of the history of heresy in church history and practical guidance as to how to understand it today, this author strongly suggests a careful reading of *Heresy: A History of Defending the Truth* by Alister McGrath (HarperCollins, 2009).

Chapter 8

1   Augustine, Confessions, trans. R. S. Pine-Coffin (Penguin, 1961), book 11, chapter 29, p. 279.

2   For example, see Isaiah 13:6, 9; Ezekiel 13:5; Amos 5:18–20; Obadiah 15; Zephaniah 1:7, 14; Malachi 4:5. For a full discussion of the use of this term by the Hebrew prophets, see "Day of the Lord," *Dictionary of the Old Testament Prophets* (IVP, 2012), pp. 132–143.

3   God declares the right to directly intervene and/or promises to do so in the future (cf. Deuteronomy 29; Psalm 96; Luke 17:20–30, 19:41–44; Philippians 1:6; 1 Thessalonians 5:1–11).

4   For example, Noah and his family (2 Peter 2:5) and Lot (2 Peter 2:7–9).

5   See Psalms 33:13–19, 147:10–11.

6   See Matthew 25:31–46, Luke 16:26, Revelation 20:11–15.

7   For warnings, see Habakkuk 2:6–19; Matthew 7:13, 23:13–39; 2 Thessalonians 1:6–10, 2:8–12.

8   See Matthew 7:14, 13:44–46; Luke 10:21–22; John 14:1–14.

Chapter 9

1   A. W. Tozer, The Knowledge of the Holy; cited from A. W. Tozer: Three Classics in One Volume (Moody, 2018), pp. 196–197.

2   2 Peter 3:10, 11, 12; Isaiah 34:4, 8–10 may imply that fire or extreme heat is the means of God's justice being poured out on the earth.

3   2 Peter 3:13; cf. Isaiah 65:17, 66:22.

4   See Revelation 21:1, 8, 27.

5   1 John 4:17; cf. 3:18–24.

6   For example, the Lord taught us to pray for the kingdom "to come on earth as it is in heaven" (Matthew 6:10); also Jesus plainly stated that testimony to Gospel would be given "to all the nations," and then the end would come (Matthew 24:14).

[7] Or to "make every effort" (cf. 1:10, 15).

[8] See Matthew 16:28–17:8; Mark 9:1–8; Luke 9:27–36.

[9] Jeremiah 23:5–7; 33:16.

[10] The apostle Paul uses the same metaphor of fire related to God's judgment and asserts that only good deeds done from genuine faith will survive this fiery purging of believers in the (not clearly defined) future before Christ (see 1 Corinthians 3:10–15).

[11] The reason for the rarity of such references is simply because the apostles' written communication was not directed to each other but to the communities of believers in the first century. Thus, we only see references when some other extraordinary circumstance occurs, in which one apostle thinks it is necessary to reference other apostles.

[12] Galatians 2:1–10; 1 Corinthians 9:3–5.

[13] Peter's matter-of-fact assertion lines up with Paul's own statements about the God-given authority he had as an apostle, and thus, logically, the authority his writings have as he speaks on behalf of God to others (cf. Romans 1:1; Galatians 1:1; 1 Corinthians 14:37; 2 Corinthians 12:19; 1 Thessalonians 2:13).

[14] Perhaps, they misused some of the slogans that Paul employed in his letters to justify their own self-indulgence (see Romans 3:8, 5:20–6:1, 7:25; 1 Corinthians 6:12–13, 8:4).

[15] The Greek term Peter uses is *strebloo*, and it was used to describe the causing of pain (torture or torment) or to twist or distort the meaning of a statement. (See *BDAG*, p. 948.)

[16] For example, Peter may have had in mind Paul's descriptions of God's patient work of salvation (see Romans 2:4; 9:19–33; Ephesians 3:1–13; Philippians 3:12–16; 1 Thessalonians 4:13–5:11; 1 Timothy 2:3–6).

[17] Jesus made this point about the Pharisees (John 5:39–47), and Paul elaborates on the inner reality of the mind dominated by sin in the light of revelation and that of believers progressively knowing the truth (Romans 8:5–7; 1 Corinthians 2:6–16).

[18] The Lord explained that this comes through faith and the presence and work of the Holy Spirit (John 6:45, 7:37–39).

[19] See 2 Peter 3:17, 2:7–8; cf. Matthew 23:28; 2 Thessalonians 2:3, 8–9; 1 Timothy 1:9; 1 John 3:4.

Afterword

[1] Henry Scougal, The Life of God in the Soul of Man (Martino Publishing, 2010), p. 69.

[2] Scougal, *The Life of God in the Soul of Man*, p. 69–70.

[3] St. John of the Cross, *Living Flame of Love*; cited from *The Collected Works of St. John of the Cross*, trans. Kieran Kavanaugh, OCD, and Otilio Rodriquez, OCD, 3rd ed. (ICS Publications, 2017), pp. 638–639.

About the Author

W. J. Caywood is a native of Arizona, a graduate of the University of Arizona with BA in Religious Studies (2000), and a graduate of Fuller Theological Seminary with a Master of Divinity (2008). He works as a Campus Minister through the Graduate and Faculty Ministry (GFM) of InterVarsity Christian Fellowship (IVCF) as well as serving as Lay Missioner within the Diocese of Western Anglicans, part of the Anglican Church in North America (ACNA).

CPSIA information can be obtained
at www.ICGtesting.com
Printed in the USA
BVHW081011060222
628232BV00006B/493